EVALUATION
FUNDAMENTALS

*E*VALUATION
*F*UNDAMENTALS

GUIDING HEALTH PROGRAMS, RESEARCH, AND POLICY

ARLENE FINK

SAGE Publications
International Educational and Professional Publisher
Newbury Park   London   New Delhi

For information address:

 SAGE Publications, Inc.
2455 Teller Road
Newbury Park, California 91320
E-mail: order@sagepub.com

SAGE Publications Ltd.
6 Bonhill Street
London EC2A 4PU
United Kingdom

SAGE Publications India Pvt. Ltd.
M-32 Market
Greater Kailash I
New Delhi 110 048 India

Printed in the United States of America

Library of Congress Cataloging-in-Publication Data

Fink, Arlene.
    Evaluation fundamentals : guiding health programs, research, and policy /
Arlene Fink.
        p.   cm.
    Includes bibliographical references and index.
        ISBN 0-8039-4838-7 (cl.) — ISBN 0-8039-4839-5 (pb.)
        1. Medical care—Evaluation.   2. Public health—Evaluation.
    I. Title.
    RA399.A1F56   1993
    362.1′068′5—dc20   93-10853

97 98 99 00 10 9 8 7 6 5

Sage Production Editor: Diane S. Foster

Brief Contents

Detailed Contents

This book is dedicated to the ones I love:
John C. Beck and, of course, Ingrid and Anja.

Preface

Over the past decade, program evaluation has made important contributions to health care practice, policy, administration, education, and research. This book explains the evaluator's goals and methods so as to provide its readers with the skills they need to review and participate in program evaluations in a health care setting.

The book has eight chapters. The chapters have been specifically organized to facilitate learning and are characterized by the following elements:

- An overview of all topics to be covered
- Learning objectives
- Textual material
- Examples of all major concepts (set off in a box)
- Separate guidelines for conducting key evaluation activities
- Forms to use in completing evaluation tasks
- Checklists
- A summary of the main ideas and topics covered in each chapter
- Exercises
- Suggested readings that cover the health field (e.g., public health, health services and policy, epidemiology, medicine, nursing)

The book also provides readers with a special scoring guide for reviewing the quality of their own and other evaluations.

The book's chapters are organized according to the main tasks involved in conducting an evaluation. These are posing evaluation questions, setting standards of effectiveness, designing the evaluation, sampling participants, selecting information sources, ensuring reliable and valid measurement, analyzing data, and reporting the results in written and oral form.

Among the special topics covered are the following:

- The use of expert panels to set standards of program effectiveness
- The literature of program evaluation, health services research, and health policy
- Qualitative evaluation methods, including participatory evaluations

- Evaluation questions, cost benefit, and cost-effectiveness
- Uses of epidemiological data and vital statistics in program evaluation
- Clinical scenarios
- Data management
- Confidence intervals
- Statistical and practical significance
- Meta-analysis
- Oral presentations (slides and transparencies)

This book is recommended for program evaluators in health and education; students and faculty in courses with content or topics in public health, public policy, health services research, and program evaluation; health program planners and administrators; health policymakers; funders of health programs; medical educators; and patient educators. The book is designed to cover the health care field and respect the needs of students in public health and the health professions as well as doctors and nurses, welfare workers, patient educators, and hospital administrators. The examples are taken from programs that include younger and older patients and cover the costs and quality of care as well as issues ranging from prevention and well-being to the care of the terminally ill.

Many people are responsible for the best parts of this book. C. Deborah Laughton of Sage was the kind of editor every author dreams of. She only deals with the relevant details and is wonderful to work with. Dr. Mark H. Beers, Steven J. Bernstein, and Helena Chmura Kraemer made important substantive contributions, and the book is much better because of their insights. Many people at Sage deserve special mention. I am most appreciative for the assistance of Diane Foster, the production editor, who had to contend with all the figures and tables. A special thank you goes to Christina Hill, who worked with the design and typesetting, and to Dick Palmer of the Design Department, and to Janet Brown, the copyeditor.

Purpose of This Chapter

The goal of this text is to provide you with the tools and skills you need to be a perceptive participant in and consumer of program evaluations. This chapter defines evaluation and discusses its purposes and methods.

1 Program Evaluation: A Prelude

A Reader's Guide to Chapter 1

What Is Program Evaluation?
  How to Evaluate: The Methods
  The Program or Intervention
  Program Merits
  Objectives and activities, outcomes, impact, and costs

Users and Doers of Evaluations

The Composition of Evaluation:
  Posing questions, setting standards, designing the study,
  sampling participants, collecting data, analyzing data, and
  reporting the results

Baseline Data, Interim Data (Formative Evaluation), and
  Process Evaluations

Qualitative Evaluation

Participatory Evaluation

Evaluation Research, Program Development, and Health
  Policy

What Is Program Evaluation?

Program evaluation is a diligent investigation of a program's characteristics and merits. Its purpose is to provide information on the effectiveness of projects so as to optimize the outcomes, efficiency, and quality of health care. Evaluations can analyze a program's structure, activities, and organization and examine its political and social environment. They can also appraise the achievement of a project's goals and objectives and the extent of its impact and costs.

HOW TO EVALUATE: THE METHODS

You do evaluations by using many of the same methods that health investigators (including clinical and health services researchers, health policy analysts, medical sociologists, and epidemiologists) rely on to gather reliable and valid evidence. Program evaluations require diligence in the choice and application of methods. These consist of formulating study questions; setting standards for establishing a program's merits; designing the evaluation; collecting data; and analyzing, interpreting, and reporting the results.

THE PROGRAM OR INTERVENTION

At the core of an evaluation is an experimental project or **program,** sometimes called an **intervention.** Programs are systematic efforts to achieve preplanned purposes such as the improvement of health, knowledge, behavior, attitudes, and practice. Programs may be relatively small (say, a health education course for seniors in two high schools, or a new community health center for persons over 75 years of age, or a campaign to vaccinate all children in a school district) or relatively large (say, Medicare, or an experiment in the regionalization of perinatal services, or a national strategy to increase public awareness of the safety of blood transfusions). Programs can take place in differing geographic and political climates and health care settings, and they vary in their purposes, structure, organization, and constituents.

PROGRAM MERITS

One of the major tasks of an evaluation is to judge a program's merits. A meritorious program has worthy goals, achieves its standards of effectiveness, provides benefits to its participants, fully informs its participants of the potential risks of participation, and does no harm. Identifying convincing evidence of program merit, measuring merit, and describing the aspects of the program that are most meritorious often distinguish evaluation from other types of health research.

PROGRAM OBJECTIVES AND ACTIVITIES

A program's objectives are its planned purposes; for example, to improve health and optimize the efficiency of the health care system. A primary function of program evaluation is to provide data on the extent to which a program's objectives are achieved. When assistance is needed in clarifying objectives or in establishing priorities among them, an evaluator might be called upon to conduct a needs assessment. A needs assessment was conducted, for example, when a director of a new family practice medical residency program in a low-income urban area asked an evaluator to conduct a systematic examination of that community's health care needs so that a curriculum to meet the needs of residents could be designed .

Evaluations also answer questions about a program's activities and offer insight into a program's implementation and management. When an evaluation focuses on the program's activities, it is termed a process evaluation. Process evaluations are important in helping to develop insights or to form hypotheses for later testing as to the reasons for the achievement (or lack of achievement) of the program's objectives. Suppose, for example, an evaluation found no differences between patient-reminder and physician-reminder programs in the number of women over 50 years of age who return each year for a mammogram. A wary evaluator would make certain to measure the extent to which each program was accomplished according to its prespecified plan. Among the questions that the evaluator could ask are these: Did all eligible patients receive reminders? All eligible physicians? How timely were the reminders?

PROGRAM OUTCOMES

The ultimate, hoped-for outcomes of health care programs include optimum health and well-being and high quality, efficient care. These outcomes are sometimes difficult to measure because of lack of consensus over their definitions and because only rarely is sufficient time available to accurately observe them. As a result, many evaluations focus on investigating the extent to which programs achieve more accessible goals and objectives. These include improvement in knowledge, attitudes, skills, and practice. The idea is that, if programs can foster the achievement of these objectives, accomplishment of the more remote outcomes is probable. The good news is that major improvements are constantly being made in the definition and measurement of health care outcomes.

PROGRAM IMPACT

Evaluations can research a program's impact, that is, the scope of its effects, the duration of its outcomes, and the extent of its influence in other health care settings and among different types of practitioners and practices. For example, consider an evaluation of two programs to improve health status.

Evaluation A concluded that Program A improved health status and that the gains were sustained for at least 3 years; moreover, when Program A was tried out in another country, participants in that country uniformly improved. Evaluation B concluded that participants in Program B also sustained improved health status for 3 years, but for fewer people; when the program was tested in another country, the evaluators noted few gains. The evaluators of Programs A and B agreed that Program A had greater impact because its benefits reached more people over a longer period of time.

PROGRAM EXPENSES AND COSTS

Evaluations are concerned with the costs of programs and their relationship to effects and benefits. Typical questions about costs are these: How efficiently is the clinic (hospital, health center) run? What are the costs of shifting care from the inpatient to the outpatient setting? For each dollar spent on a monthly home visit by a nurse practitioner, how much is saved in terms of future hospitalizations and visits to a physician?

Users and Doers of Evaluations

Information from evaluations is used by at least five different groups:

- federal, state, and local government (for example, a city, county, or state department of health or the National Institutes of Health)
- program developers (for example, a director of a community health clinic or a nursing school's curriculum committee)
- health policymakers (for example, a subcommittee on the health of the state or federal legislature, or the people who make decisions regarding how much to reimburse physicians)
- program funders (for example, the institutes of the National Institutes of Health and philanthropic foundations)
- health researchers (in government, business, public agencies, and universities)

Evaluations are sometimes conducted by teams of individuals, each of whom contributes expertise. Consider the evaluations described in Example 1.1:

Example 1.1: Program Evaluation as an Interdisciplinary Discipline

- A 4-year evaluation of a new program in ambulatory care depended upon a team of two professional evaluators, a sociologist, a survey researcher, and two physicians. Consultants included a nurse, an economist, and trained data collectors.

- A 3-year evaluation of a 35-project program to improve access to and use of prenatal care for low-income women relied on a professional evaluator, an epidemiologist, a nurse practitioner, and an economist.

- An evaluation of a newly developed questionnaire for office-based physicians to use in measuring patients' social, psychological, and physical functioning relied on four physicians, an evaluator, a psychometrician, and an occupational therapist.

- An evaluation of a program using nurses to screen community-dwelling elderly for hypertension, vision, and hearing disorders relied on two physicians and an evaluator.

The Composition of Program Evaluation

Program evaluations typically consist of the following activities:

1. posing questions about the program,
2. setting standards of effectiveness,
3. designing the evaluation and selecting participants,
4. collecting data,
5. analyzing data, and
6. reporting the results.

1. POSING EVALUATION QUESTIONS

The combined answers to evaluation questions are a primary basis for judging a program's merits. Typical evaluation questions are as follows:

- To what extent did the program achieve its goals and objectives?
- What are the characteristics of the individuals and groups who participated in the program?
- For which individuals or groups was the program most effective?
- How enduring were the effects?
- Which features (e.g., activities, settings, management strategies) of the program were most effective?
- How applicable are the program's objectives and activities to other participants in other settings?
- What are the relationships among the costs of the program and its effects?
- To what extent did changes in social, political, and financial circumstances influence the program's support and outcomes?

2. SETTING STANDARDS OF EFFECTIVENESS

Setting standards means deciding on the information needed to provide convincing evidence of a program's effectiveness, an important component of an evaluator's appraisal of merit. For example, consider these possible standards for the objective "to improve children's dietary and other health habits":

- testimony from children (parents, and teachers) in the program that their habits had improved
- observations by the evaluator of improved health habits (e.g., through studies of choices of sracks during and between meals)
- physical examinations by a nurse practitioner revealing evidence of children's improved health status
- a difference in habits and health status favoring children who are in the program when compared with children who are not

The challenge to the evaluator is to identify standards that are appropriate for the program, possible to measure, and credible.

3. DESIGNING THE EVALUATION AND SELECTING PARTICIPANTS

Evaluation design refers to the manner in which the environment is structured so that any documented effects that seem to have resulted from the program can be conclusively linked to it. Standard evaluation designs include comparing one group's performance over time and comparing two groups at one or many times. For example, suppose five universities plan to participate in an evaluation of a new program to teach the basic principles of evaluation research to Health Corps trainees. The evaluation will have to decide on such issues as whether some or all universities should receive the program, how many times Health Corps trainees should be tested to determine the extent of learning, and when they should be tested (Before and after each lesson? Before and after the program? How long after the program?).

Among the general questions asked by evaluators when considering the design of their study are these:

- How many measurements should I make?
- When should the measurements be made?
- How many institutions, groups, or persons should be included in the evaluation?
- How should the institutions, groups, or persons be chosen?

4. COLLECTING DATA

The collection of evaluation information is really a set of tasks that include the following:

- identifying the variables to measure (e.g., the specific knowledge, performance, attitudes, or behaviors that are the focus of the program's objectives)
- selecting, adapting, or creating measures
- demonstrating the reliability (consistency) and validity (accuracy) of the
  measures
- administering the measure
- scoring and interpreting the results

Some common sources of evaluation data are as follows:

- literature reviews
- performance tests (including "standardized patients")
- medical record reviews
- existing data bases such as epidemiological records (e.g., morbidity and
  mortality statistics)
- self-administered questionnaires
- interviews
- achievement tests
- direct observations
- physical examinations
- clinical scenarios

5. ANALYZING DATA

The choice of which method of analysis to use is dependent upon
considerations such as these:

- the characteristics of the evaluation question and standards (Do they ask
  about differences or associations over time among groups? Costs and effects?
  Use of services?)
- how the variables are expressed: nominally (e.g., qualitative or categorical
  such as: did or did not receive a flu shot); ordinally (Stage I, II, or III of a
  disease); or numerically (scores on an interval scale of physical function)
- the number of measures
- the reliability and validity of the data

6. REPORTING THE RESULTS

An evaluation report consists of descriptions of a program's characteristics and explanations as well as judgments of its merits. The report
describes the purposes of the evaluation, presents the methods (including
the standard-setting process, research design, sampling, data collection, and
analysis) and results, and discusses the program and the implications of the
results. Evaluation reports may be oral or written as books, monographs, or
articles.

Baseline Data, Interim Data (Formative Evaluation), and Process Evaluations

Evaluations are conducted to find out the extent to which an an intervention or program is effective and efficient in influencing health outcomes and the organization and quality of care. The evaluator typically assumes that the program is needed and that a program protocol has been prepared to meet the needs. If the assumptions are erroneous, and the evaluation continues, the results will necessarily be invalid.

The need for the program is demonstrated by collecting data to show that the participants start out with one or more difficulties that are in need of an intervention. These baseline data provide facts regarding the participants' condition before the program. Interim data, which are collected during the course of the program, provide information on the program's progress in meeting the needs of the participants.

BASELINE DATA

Baseline data are collected before the start of the program. Suppose you are to evaluate a program that is being planned to instruct physicians in the use of a new set of guidelines for treating problems like depression and hypertension. A review of a sample of patients' medical records can assist you in determining the extent to which physicians are already using the guidelines. If you find evidence that all physicians are already using the guidelines, you can assume that the program is not needed.

Baseline data are often collected to describe the characteristics of participants (such as their health status and demographic features) that are important later on in interpreting the effects of the program. Example 1.2 illustates some of the reasons program evaluators collect baseline data.

Example 1.2: Baseline Data and Program Evaluation

The Agency for Health Care Policy and Research has published extensive guidelines for identifying and treating hypertensive patients. An evaluation of the effectiveness of the guidelines is being conducted nationally. Before the evaluators begin the formal process of evaluation, they will collect baseline data on the extent to which physicians in differing health care settings (such as health maintenance organizations and private group practices) already follow the practices recommended by the guidelines; the prevalence of hypertension in the community; and the number of hypertensive patients that are likely to be seen in the evaluation's proposed duration of 3 years.

INTERIM DATA OR FORMATIVE EVALUATION

Interim data (sometimes called "formative evaluation") are reported after the start of a program, but before its conclusion, say 18 months after the beginning of a 3-year intervention. Their purposes are to describe the progress of the program and of the evaluation.

Because interim data are always preliminary, you must always interpret them cautiously. Example 1.3 is an illustration of the need for taking care in interpreting preliminary, formative findings.

Example 1.3: Formative Evaluation and Interim Data: Proceed With Care

In a 3-year study of access to prenatal care, the results of a 14-month formative evaluation found that three of six community clinics had opened on schedule and were providing health services to needy women exactly as planned. Preliminary data also revealed that 200 women had been served in the clinics and that the percentage of babies born weighing less than 2,500 grams (5.5 pounds) was 4%, well below the state's average of 6%. The evaluation concluded that progress was definitely being made toward improving access to prenatal care. After 3 years, the evaluation results were quite different, however. The remaining three clinics were never opened, and one of the original three was closed. Many fewer women were served than anticipated, and the percentage of low birth weight babies was 6.6%.

Accordingly, although formative evaluations and interim data may sometimes appear to be useful, they also may be misleading; further, they are extremely expensive to conduct. With relatively short programs—say, 2 years or less—they are probably not very useful at all. Some evaluators will not participate in studies of interventions that are not carefully defined and standardized (and therefore not in need of formative evaluation), suggesting that such analyses belong to the program developers. Consider Example 1.4:

Example 1.4: Questions Asked in a Formative Evaluation of a Program for Critically Ill Children

Many experts agree that the emergency medical services needed by critically ill and injured children differ in important ways from those needed by adults. As a result, a number of states have attempted to reorganize their emergency services to provide

→

Example 1.4 (Continued)

better care to children. One state commissioned a 3-year evaluation of its program. It was specifically concerned with the characteristics and effectiveness of its about-to-be implemented intervention to improve transfers from adult inpatient or intensive care units and to maximize quality of care for children with cardiopulmonary arrest in the emergency department and in intensive care units.

In planning the evaluation, the evaluators decided to check a sample of medical records in 15 of the state's 56 counties to see whether sufficient information was available to use the records as a main source of data. Also, the evaluators planned to release preliminary findings after 12 months. This would involve reviews of records as well as interviews with physicians, hospital administrators, paramedics, and families. An expert's review of the evaluation raised these questions:

1. Although the evaluation is a "3-year evaluation," does that mean 3 years of data collection? How much time will you need to plan the evaluation?

2. Interim data have been promised in a year. Can you develop and validate medical record review forms in time to collect enough information to present meaningful findings?

3. Can you develop, validate, and administer the survey forms in the time available?

4. To what extent will the interim and preliminary analysis answer the same or similar questions? If they are very different, will you have sufficient time and money to do both well?

5. Will a written or oral interim report be required?

PROCESS EVALUATIONS

A process evaluation is concerned with the extent to which planned activities are executed, and its findings may be reported upon at any time. Process evaluations are nearly always useful. In a randomized trial of three interventions to increase the rates at which women returned to follow-up on their abnormal Pap smears, for example, a process evaluation concluded that implementation of the intervention protocols was less than perfect and thus introduced a conservative bias into the results of the outcome evaluation. Consider Example 1.5:

Example 1.5: Process Evaluation: Follow-up of Abnormal Pap Smears

During the course of the 2-year evaluation, all women were to be surveyed at least once regarding whether they had received the program and the extent to which they understood its purposes and adhered to its requirements. Telephone interviews after 18 months revealed that 74 of 100 women (74%) in the slide-tape intervention had seen the entire

→

Example 1.5 (Continued)

25-minute presentation; 70 of 111 (63%) had received mailed reminders from their physicians' offices to come back for another Pap smear; and 32 of 101 (about 32%) had received phone calls from their physicians' offices. These findings helped explain the apparent failure of the third intervention to achieve positive results when compared with the other two.

Qualitative Evaluation

Qualitative evaluations collect data from in-person interviews, direct observations, and written documents (such as private diaries). These evaluations aim to provide personalized information on the dynamics of a program and on participants' perceptions of their outcomes and impact. Qualitative evaluation methods are useful for a program whose goals are in the process of being defined and to test out the workability of the evaluation's methods. Because they are "personalized," qualitative methods may add emotion and tone to purely statistical findings and provide a means of gauging outcomes when reliable and valid measures of those outcomes are unlikely to become available in time for the evaluation report.

Qualitative methods are employed in program evaluations to complement the usual sources of data (such as standardized surveys and medical record reviews, physical examinations, and achievement tests). Example 1.6 illustates some of the uses of qualitative information in program evaluation:

Example 1.6: Uses of Qualitative Methods in Program Evaluation

1. To evaluate the effectiveness of a campaign to get heroin addicts to clean their needles with Clorox, the evaluators spend time in a heroin "shooting gallery." Although they bring a tape recorder with them, they rarely use it. They find that, although needles are being cleaned, a common dish is used to rinse needles and dilute the drug before shooting. A recommendation is made to alter the community's program to recognize the dangers of using the common dish.

Comment: The evaluators are observers of the shooting gallery. They do not conduct systematic surveys of the participants in the gallery.

2. To evaluate the effectiveness of an education-counseling program for mentally ill adults, the evaluation team lives for 3 months in five different residential communities. After taping more than 250 counseling sessions, the evaluators conclude that the quality varies greatly both within and among the communities, helping to explain the overall program's inconsistent results.

→

Example 1.6 (Continued)

Comment: The evaluators tape the sessions and then interpret the results. The interpretations come after the data are collected; no effort is made to postulate advance hypotheses.

3. To evaluate the impact of a school-based health program for homeless children, the evaluators teach a cohort of children to keep diaries over a 3-year period. The evaluation finds that children in the program are much more willing to attend to the dangers of smoking and other drug use than children in schools without the program. The diaries reveal that children in the program are especially pleased to participate. The evaluators conclude that the children's enjoyment may be related to the program's positive outcomes.

Comment: The use of diaries is a primary qualitative tool. It allows participants to say how they feel in their own words.

4. An evaluation of the impact on the county of a program to improve access to and use of prenatal care services asks "opinion leaders" to give their views. These people are known in the county to have expertise in providing, financing, and evaluating prenatal care. The interviewers encourage the leaders to bring up any issues that concern them. These people reveal that improvements are probably due to medical advances rather than to access to services. After the interviews are completed, the evaluators conclude that major barriers to access and use continue to exist even though statistical registries reveal a decline in the infant mortality rate for some groups of women.

Comment: The experts are invited to give their own views; little attempt is made to oblige the opinion leaders to adhere to certain topics.

Participatory Evaluation

A participatory evaluation invites representatives of groups who will be affected by the study's results to join the evaluation team for certain activities. These may include selecting evaluation questions, setting standards, choosing measures, and keeping the evaluator up-to-date on daily activities. Participatory evaluations can be very helpful in educating people who are not familiar with the evaluation process, in enlisting their support in data collection, and in adding meaning to statistical findings. Participatory evaluations are not without limitations, however. They require the evaluator to have skills in working with disparate groups of people, and they need time and patience.

Evaluation Research, Program Development, and Health Policy

Program evaluation has traditionally been viewed as a method of systematically collecting and analyzing data about a specific program to improve or sum its overall performance. Over the past few decades, however, this insular perspective on the purposes of evaluation has evolved into a more global one, particularly in the field of health care.

Since the 1980s, program evaluation has assumed a prominent position as a key component of health services research. In part, this is due to improvements in its methods, but the field has also attracted practitioners with expertise in scientifically analyzing interventions so that health program developers, researchers, and policymakers have access to a continually growing quantity of empirically based evidence.

No longer do evaluators have to tiptoe behind program developers and funders, hoping for permission to collect data. Evaluation has proven its usefulness to the extent that most federal and state programs require evaluations of new programs, and some health foundations hire staff specifically to oversee evaluation activities. In addition, evaluations are newsworthy. On a single day—April 23, 1992—page 1 of *The New York Times* featured two evaluations: an evaluation of a U.S. program linking welfare payments to job training and an evaluation of the impact on children's knowledge of current events with the use of commercial in-school television.

Despite the maturation of evaluation methods and uses and interest in their findings, some evaluation practitioners continue to assert that their discipline is only rarely a form of research. These practitioners claim that, at certain stages of program development, research of any kind is neither practical nor even desirable. The argument usually given to defend this view is that of a newly organized program that needs time to grow and train its staff and whose goals and objectives are evolving. During the beginnings of any new program, evaluators may be called in to help reformulate the goals and reassess the validity of the original standards; research is irrelevant. Further, the argument continues, evaluators are sometimes asked to conduct "summative" evaluations. These are historical reviews of programs that take place after they have been in operation for some period of time, and they are performed so that already developed and "evaluatable" programs can be summed up and compared. Evaluatable programs are those that are in full operation.

The argument that evaluation is rarely, if ever, research is flawed because it assumes that evaluators are really program developers at the mercy of a "real" world that is inimical to research. It is true that some trained evaluators have the skills to participate in program development, monitoring, and review, and that practical concerns sometimes render research difficult to pursue. It is nonetheless more likely, however, that graduates of disciplines that are directly concerned with institutional organization and management are better trained in program development than are evaluators. Evaluators are likely to be most helpful and influential in providing scientific data that are applicable beyond the needs of a single intervention.

Evaluation is useful to policymakers only if it is a scientific endeavor with generalizable results. "Policymakers" regulate education in, access to, delivery of, and reimbursement for health care. They may be legislators, insurers, philanthropic foundation leaders, and health educators. They can have little use for data on the specific issues that pertain to the implementation of a single program, the hiring and training of its staff, and the perfection of its goals and standards.

Health researchers, too, benefit little if evaluators focus their efforts on arbitrarily selected testimony and uncontrolled case studies of single programs. Current researchers want to learn more about high-quality health care and how to deliver and appraise it. The most constructive way of providing valid data on quality, effectiveness, efficiency, and methods is to use scientific procedures to investigate programs. The ability to do this is the unique provenance of the program evaluator.

SUMMARY AND TRANSITION TO THE NEXT CHAPTER ON QUESTIONS AND STANDARDS

Evaluation is a diligent investigation of a program's characteristics and merits. Its purpose is to provide information on a program's objectives, activities, outcomes, impact, and cost. To conduct an evaluation means posing questions and setting standards for effectiveness, deciding on the design and sampling, and collecting, analyzing, interpreting, and reporting information. Evaluation information is used by financial supporters of health programs, program developers, policymakers, and other evaluators and health researchers. Collecting interim or formative evaluation data may be misleading and expensive; proceed with caution. Process evaluations are usually useful.

Before deciding on the types of data to collect for an evaluation and the design for collecting them, the evaluator must decide on the evaluation questions and the standards by which program effectiveness will be appraised. The next chapter discusses the sources and statement of evaluation questions and standards. The chapter also explains where standards of program effectiveness come from and describes the principles behind the use of expert panels, a commonly used method of coming to agreement on standards. Experts are often used in health and medicine to resolve the controversy surrounding the uncertainty associated with issues in health, and they are particularly useful in setting standards when statistical methods alone are insufficient.

EXERCISE: PROGRAM EVALUATION:
A PRELUDE

Directions

Read the example below and, using only the information offered, answer these questions:

1. What are the evaluation questions?
2. What are the standards?
3. What is the design?
4. What data collection measures are being used?
5. What additional information do you need to perform the evaluation?

Exercise: An Evaluation of a Geriatrics Education Program

The Huntington-Ball University is concerned with improving its education in geriatrics and gerontology and is planning to revise its entire curriculum in that area, starting with geriatric medicine. The improvements are to take place over a 3-year period. The evaluation team convenes a panel of nurses, physicians, pharmacists, and social workers to help identify the key curriculum objectives that should be evaluated. Based on the panel's suggestions, as well as reviews of the current and proposed curriculum and of the published literature, the evaluation team decides on a plan of action. Each year, they will test all third- and fourth-year medical students and survey all residents and a sample of faculty physicians to ascertain their knowledge. The evaluation team also plans to conduct medical record reviews to determine the quality of care delivered to patients between 65 and 75 years of age, 76 to 85, and over 85. Student achievement and quality of care will be monitored over time. The evaluator will also be investigating whether the curriculum is equally successful for students, residents, and faculty and if any observed improvements are sustained over time. A report will be available 6 months after the conclusion of the program.

Suggested Readings

General

Ginzberg, E. (Ed.). (1991). *Health services research*. Cambridge, MA: Harvard University Press.

A report from the Foundation for Health Services Research, which discusses a number of economic and policy questions that are also of concern to health program evaluators. See especially chapter 7, written by Joseph P. Newhouse, "Controlled Experimentation as Research Policy." Dr. Newhouse discusses in detail the RAND Health Insurance Experiment, which was a decade-long multimillion-dollar controlled trial in health-care financing.

Holden, C. (1989). Street-wise crack research. *Science, 246,* 1376-1381.

Tells of the use of ethnographic ("qualitative") methods in collecting behavioral data on "crack families."

Kosecoff, J., & Fink, A. (1982). *Evaluation basics*. Beverly Hills, CA: Sage.

Gives an overview of the methods and purposes of the methods and purposes of program evaluation.

Patton, M. Q. (1987). *How to use qualitative methods in evaluation*. Newbury Park, CA: Sage.

Tells when to use qualitative methods, how to design qualitative evaluations, discusses fieldwork and observation, in-depth interviewing, and how to analyze and interpret qualitative data.

Rossi, P. H., & Freeman, H. E. (1993). *Evaluation: A systematic approach*. Newbury Park, CA: Sage.

A basic text on the context and purposes of evaluation. An excellent discussion on cost-benefit and cost-effectiveness evaluation.

Satcher, D., Kosecoff, J., & Fink A. (1980). The results of a needs assessment in planning a family practice center and residency program. *Journal of Family Practice, 10,* 871-879.

An example of the use of a needs assessment to define objectives for a family practice residency in an urban community.

Examples of Program Evaluations in the Health Professions

Brook, R. H., Fink, A., Kosecoff, J., et al. (1987). Educating physicians and treating patients in the ambulatory setting. Where are we going and how will we know when we arrive? *Annals of Internal Medicine, 107,* 392-398.

Brook, R. H., Ware, J. E., Rogers W. H., et al. (1983). Does free care improve adults' health? Results from a randomized controlled trial. *New England Journal of Medicine 309,* 1426-1434.

Brooten, D., Kumar, S., Brown, L., et al. (1986). A randomized clinical trial of early hospital discharge and home follow-up of very-low birth-weight infants. *New England Journal of Medicine, 315,* 934-938.

Elster, A., Lamb, M., Tavare, J., et al. (1987). The medical and psychosocial impact of comprehensive care on adolescent pregnancy and parenthood. *Journal of the American Medical Association, 258,* 1187-1192.

Goodman, L. J., Brueschke, R. C., Bone, W. H., et al. (1991). An experiment in medical education. *Journal of the American Medical Association, 265,* 2373-2376.

Gunn, J., Shapiro, S., et al. (1991). Health care use among young children in day care: Results in a randomized trial of early intervention. *Journal of the American Medical Association, 265,* 2212-2217.

Kosecoff, J., Fink, A., Brook, R. H., et al. (1985). General medical care and the education of internists in university hospitals: An evaluation of the Teaching Hospital General Medicine Group Practice Program. *Annals of Internal Medicine, 102,* 250-257.

Lomas, J., Enkin, M., Anderson, G. M., et al. (1991). Opinion leaders vs. audit and feedback to implement practice guidelines: Delivery after previous cesarean section. *Journal of the American Medical Association, 265,* 2202-2207.

Marcus, A. C., Crane, L. A., Kaplan, C. P., et al. (1992). Improving adherence to screening follow-up among women with abnormal Pap smears: Results from a large clinic-based trial of three intervention strategies. *Medical Care, 30,* 216-228.

Pollack, M. M., Getson, P. R., Ruttimann, U. E., Steinhart, C. M., Kanter, R. K., Katz, R. W., et al. (1987). A comparative analysis of eight pediatric intensive care units. *Journal of the American Medical Association, 258,* 1481-1486.

Rubenstein, L. V., Calkins, D. R., Young, R. T., et al. (1989). Improving patient function: A randomized trial of functional disability screening. *Annals of Internal Medicine, 111,* 836-842.

Sulmasy, D. P., Geller, G., Faden, R., & Levine, D. (1992). The quality of mercy: Caring for patients with "Do not resuscitate orders." *Journal of the American Medical Association, 267,* 682-686.

Purpose of This Chapter

This chapter explains the characteristics of evaluation questions and discusses how to set standards. It explains the major purpose of evaluation questions, which is to provide data on the characteristics and merits of programs. The standards are the criteria for appraising effectiveness. They can be set statistically, but the evaluator must be careful to check them for practical meaning. The chapter also reviews the special role of experts in setting standards. Experts can provide insights into practical meaning when data alone are unavailable or insufficient. The relationships among evaluation questions and standards and the independent and dependent variables are also examined and summarized in a chart that visually depicts the connections.

2 Evaluation Questions and Standards

Evaluation Questions: Goals and Objectives

Evaluation questions provide data on a program's characteristics and merits. In most evaluations, a main concern is to find out if a program's goals and objectives have been met. The goals are usually meant to be relatively general and long term, as shown in Example 2.1.

Example 2.1: Typical Program Goals

For the Public
  Optimize their health status
  Improve their quality of life
  Foster their improved physical, social,
    and psychological functioning
  Support new knowledge for them about
    health care
  Enhance their satisfaction with care

For Health Care Practitioners
  Promote their research
  Enhance their knowledge
  Support their access to new technol-
    ogy and practices
  Improve their quality of care
  Improve their education

For Health Care Practitioners (Continued)
  Foster their delivery of efficient care

For Institutions
  Improve their organization, structure,
    and efficiency
  Optimize their ability to deliver access-
    ible high-quality care and superior
    education

For the Health Care System
  Expand its capacity to provide high-
    quality care
  Support its ability to provide efficient
    care
  Ensure its respect for the health-care
    needs of all citizens

Objectives refer to the specific purposes that a program plans to achieve. Consider these excerpts from the description of a new course given in Example 2.2:

Example 2.2: The Objectives of a New Course

The new two-semester course is designed to teach first- and second-year graduate students to conduct evaluations of health programs. Among the primary aims is to develop a handbook on evaluation that teaches students the basic principles of evaluation and offers an annotated bibliography so that more information can be obtained, when needed. At the end of the two semesters, students will be expected to plan the evaluation of a program. The plan is to include evaluation questions, standards, study design and sampling methods, and data collection measures.

Based on this excerpt, the objectives are as follows:

For the curriculum developer:

♦ To produce an evaluation handbook with an annotated bibliography

For the student:

♦ To prepare an evaluation plan that includes questions, standards, research design, sampling methods, and data collection measures

Objectives can be aimed at any of the users or participants in the evaluation: patients, students, and health care practitioners, the system, and so on. The evaluation questions for the health program evaluation course might include the following:

1. Was a health program evaluation handbook produced?
2. Did students prepare an evaluation plan with questions, standards, study design, sampling, and data collection measures?

The identification of these two questions immediately raises some additional questions. By when should the handbook be produced? How will we determine if it is any good? What are the characteristics of a satisfactory evaluation plan, and who will judge it? How many students must prepare a satisfactory evaluation plan? These questions must be answered in subsequent evaluation activities. In the next step of the evaluation, for example, we will consider ways of setting standards for determining achievement of objectives and program effectiveness and efficiency.

When identifying evaluation questions based on goals and objectives, the evaluator must be certain that all important goals and objectives have been identified, that the evaluation questions cover all important objectives, and that all questions can be answered with the resources available.

Evaluation Questions:
Participants and Effectiveness

Evaluation questions often aim to describe the demographic and health characteristics of participants in a program and to link effective outcomes to specific participants. An evaluator might be asked, for example, to find out whether a diabetes education program was effective with all patients or only a portion—say, patients under 18 years of age. Returning to the new health program evaluation course, consider the questions in Example 2.3 about the program's participants:

Example 2.3: Evaluation Questions, Participants, and Program Effectiveness

The new health program evaluation course for first- and second-year students was concerned with finding out if the program was effective for all types of students. One measure of effectiveness is the student's ability to prepare a satisfactory evaluation plan. The evaluator asked the following evaluation questions:

- What are the demographic characteristics of each year's students?

- Is the program equally effective for differing students (for example, males and females)?
- Do first- and second-year students differ in their learning?
- At the end of their second year, do the current group of first-year students maintain their learning?

Previously, we made the point that evaluation questions should be answerable with the resources available. Suppose that the evaluation were only a one-year study. If that were the case, then the evaluator could not answer the question regarding whether this year's first-year students maintained their learning over the next year. Practical considerations often temper the ambitions of an evaluation.

Evaluation Questions: Program Activities, Organization, and Effectiveness

Learning about a program's specific activities and its organization is frequently important in understanding its success or failure and if it is applicable to other settings. Typical questions that focus on the program's activities are these:

- What were the key activities?
- To what extent were the activities implemented as planned?
- How well was the program administered?
- Did the program's influence carry over to other programs? Institutions? Consumers?
- Did social, political, or financial circumstances change so as to influence the effectiveness of the program?

Consider the case study in Example 2.4, in which specific questions are posed about program activities and organization:

Example 2.4: Evaluation Questions, Activities, and Organization

A nine-member panel of experts in public health, nursing, health services research, and evaluation met to define the kinds of learning that are appropriate for a course in health program evaluation. The course's evaluation is to take place over a 4-year period so as to enlist two groups of first- and second-year students. Several of the best instructors were selected to help design the curriculum and the handbook and to teach the course. The evaluator asks:

- To what extent is the selection of the best teachers responsible for the quality of student learning and of the handbook?
- Does the new course affect students' subsequent education activities?
- Over the 4-year period of the evaluation, do any changes occur in the school's support for the program or the number and types of faculty who were willing to participate?

Evaluation Questions: Economics and Costs

Program evaluations can be designed to answer questions about the resources that are consumed to produce program outcomes. The resources—costs—may be money, personnel, equipment, time, and facilities (e.g., office equipment and buildings). The outcomes may be monetary (e.g., the number of dollars saved) or substantive (e.g., better functioning). When questions focus on the relationship between costs and monetary outcomes, the evaluation is termed a "cost-benefit analysis." When questions are asked about the relationship between costs and substantive outcomes, the evaluation is called a "cost-effectiveness evaluation."

Cost-effectiveness. What are the comparative costs of Programs A and B in providing the means for women to obtain prenatal care during the first trimester?

Cost-benefit. For every $100 spent on prenatal care, how much is saved on neonatal intensive care?

Questions about costs are asked relatively infrequently in evaluations for a number of reasons. Among them are difficulties in defining costs and measuring benefits. Experts disagree about the best analytic methods to use to answer cost questions and if an analysis ought to be conducted as part of the overall evaluation or as a separate study. When conducted concurrently, the economic analysis may add additional complexities to an already complex evaluation design; also, studying the costs of an intervention of (as yet) unproven effectiveness may not be warranted. Separate analyses, however, have the disadvantage of requiring a potentially different, second study.

Example 2.5 illustrates the types of questions that program evaluators pose about the costs, effects, benefits, and efficiency of health care.

Example 2.5: Evaluation Questions: Costs

1. What is the relationship between the cost and effectiveness of three prenatal clinic staffing models: physician based, mixed staffing, and clinical nurse specialists with physicians available for consultation? Costs include number of staff, hourly wages, number of prenatal appointments made and kept, and number of hours spent delivering prenatal care. Outcomes (effectiveness) include maternal health (such as complications at the time of delivery); neonatal health (such as birth weight); and patient satisfaction.

2. How efficient are the ambulatory clinics? Efficiency is defined as the relationship between the use of practitioner time and the size of a clinic, waiting times for appointments, time spent by faculty in the clinic, and time spent supervising house staff.

3. How do the most profitable practices differ from the least profitable in terms of types of ownership, collection rates, no-show rates, percentage of patients without insur-ance coverage, charge for a typical follow-up visit, space occupancy rates, and practitioner costs?

4. To what extent does each of three programs to control hypertension produce an annual savings in reduced health care claims that is greater than the annual cost of operating the program? The benefits are costs per hypertensive client (the costs of operating the program in each year, divided by the number of hypertensive employees being monitored and counseled that year). Because estimates of program costs are produced over a given 2-year period, but estimates of savings are produced in a different (later) period, benefits have to be adjusted to a standard year. To do this, the total claims paid in each calendar year are adjusted by the consumer price index for medical care costs to a standard 1993 dollar. The costs of operating the programs are similarly adjusted to 1993 dollars, using the same index.

As can be seen from these questions, costs and effectiveness or benefits must be defined, and, when appropriate, the value of the monetary costs must be described. Evaluators who answer questions about the costs of health programs sometimes perform a "sensitivity analysis" when measures are not precise or the estimates are uncertain. Suppose that in a study of the comparative cost-effectiveness of two state-funded school-based health care programs, the evaluators analyze the influence of increasing each program's funding first by 5% and then by 10%. In this case, the evaluators are testing the "sensitivity" of the program's effectiveness to changes in funding level. With this analysis, the evaluators will be able to tell if increases in measures of effectiveness keep pace with increases in costs.

Evaluation Questions: Program Environment

All programs take place in institutional, social, and political environments. Program A, which aims to improve the preventive health care practices of children under 14, for example, takes place in rural schools and is funded by the federal government and the state. Program B has the same aim; however, it takes place in a large city and is supported by the city and a private foundation.

If an evaluation takes place over several years (say, 3 or more), the social or political environment can change. New people and policies may emerge, and these may influence the program and the evaluation. Environmental changes that have affected programs in health care include alterations in reimbursement policies for hospitals and physicians, discoveries of new technology, and advances in medical science. For example, the decrease in the infant mortality rate seen in the United States from 1980 to 1990 is generally conceded to be the result of programs in prenatal care as well as increases in Medicaid spending for prenatal care, medical advances in treating the underdeveloped lungs of infants in their first hours of life, and other means of neonatal intensive care.

When evaluating the program's environment, consider collecting data on the program's setting and funding as illustrated in Figure 2.1, page 26.

In addition to asking questions about a program's settings and funding, questions about program management and politics are also relevant:

- The managerial structure. Who is responsible for the program's outcomes? How effective is the managerial structure? If the individuals or groups who are running the program were to leave, would the program continue to be effective?
- The political context. Is the political environment (meaning within or outside the institution) supportive of the success of the program? Is the program well funded?

Setting Standards: What They Are and How to State Them

Program evaluations aim to provide convincing evidence that a program is effective. The standards are the specific criteria by which effectiveness is measured. Consider the following evaluation questions and their associated standards:

Evaluation question: Did students learn to formulate evaluation questions?

Standard: Of all students in the new program, 90% will learn to formulate evaluation questions. Learning to formulate questions means identifying and justifying program goals and objectives and benefits and stating the question

Program/Intervention Settings

Type of setting(s):   [ ] Community hospital clinic
(check all that apply) [ ] Community freestanding clinic
                        [ ] Community physicians' office
                        [ ] Academic hospital clinic
                        [ ] Residential treatment facility
                        [ ] Private residence
                        [ ] Other facility type not shown above, specify:

                        _____

                        _____

Geographic location(s):

A. Country: B. State(s):   C. Local (e.g., county/city)
    [ ] U.S.   1. ___ ___   1. _____
    [ ] European   2. ___ ___   (enter up to   2. _____
    [ ] Other, specify: 3. ___ ___   five different   3. _____
                              4. ___ ___   state codes or   4. _____
    _____   5. ___ ___   abbreviations)   5. _____
    _____   [ ] CHECK HERE   [ ] CHECK HERE
                                 IF STUDY USED   IF STUDY
                                 >5 STATES   USED >5
                                                          CITIES/
                                                          COUNTIES

Funding Source(s):   [ ] Federal government, specify:_____
(check all that apply) [ ] State government, specify:_____
                        [ ] Local government (county/city), specify:____
                        [ ] Private foundation, specify:_____
                        [ ] Other, specify:_____
                        [ ] None stated

Figure 2.1. A Form to Survey the Program's Environment

in a comprehensible manner. Evidence that the questions are comprehensible will come from review by at least three potential users of the evaluation.

AND

Evaluation question: Did the current group of first-year students maintain their learning by the end of their second year?

Standard: No decreases in learning will be found between second and first years.

In this case, unless 90% of students learn to formulate questions by the end of the first year **and** first-year students maintain their learning over time, the evaluator cannot say the program is effective.

The standards are the key to the evaluation's credibility. The more specific they are, the easier they are to measure. To get at specificity, all potentially ambiguous terms in the evaluation questions and standards must be defined. Ambiguity arises when uniformly accepted definitions or levels of performance are unavailable. In the evaluation question, "Has the Obstetrical Access and Utilization Initiative improved access to prenatal care for high-risk women?" improved access to prenatal care and high-risk are potentially ambiguous terms. To clarify the ambiguity, a dialogue like the one illustrated in Example 2.6 is helpful.

Example 2.6: Dialogue Between Evaluators in Clarifying Terms and Setting Standards

Evaluator 1: "Improved" means bettered or corrected.

Evaluator 2: For how many women and over what duration of time must care be bettered? Will all women be included? Or 90% of all women, but 100% of teens?

Evaluator 1: "Access" means more available and convenient care.

Evaluator 2: What might render care more available and convenient? Care can be made more available and convenient if some or all the following occur: changes in the health care system to include the provision of services relatively close to home; shorter waiting times at clinics; for some women, financial help, assistance being transported to care, and aid with child care; and education regarding the benefits of prenatal care and compliance with nutrition advice.

Evaluator 1: "High-risk" women are those whose health and birth outcomes have a higher than average chance of being poor.

Evaluator 2: Which, if not all, of the following women will you include? Teens? Users of drugs or alcohol? Smokers? Low-income women? Women with health problems such as gestational diabetes or hypertension?

After clarifying terms, the evaluator might come up with standards such as those given in Example 2.7 for the question, "Has the Obstetrical Access and Utilization Initiative improved access to prenatal care for high-risk women?"

Example 2.7: Illustrative Standards for Access to and Use of Prenatal Care Services

- At least four classes in nutrition and "how to be a parent" will be implemented, especially for teenagers.
- All clinics will provide translation assistance in English, Spanish, Hmong, and Vietnamese.

- Over a 5-year period, 80% of all women without transportation to clinics and community health centers will receive it.

Notice that the three standards refer to changes in the structure of health care: provision of specially designed education, translation assistance, and transportation. A useful way to think about standards is to decide whether you want to measure the program's effectiveness in terms of the "structure," "process," or "outcomes" of health care. These three terms are often used in program evaluation as a way of conceptualizing the quality of care.

The **structure of care** refers to the environment in which health care is given and refers to the characteristics of the health care practitioners (including the number of practitioners and their educational and demographic backgrounds); setting (fee-for-service or managed care, for example); and organization of care (for example, how departments and teams are run).

The **process of care** means what is done to and for patients and includes the technical and humanistic aspects of care. The processes include the procedures and tests used by the health care team in prevention, diagnosis, treatment, and rehabilitation.

The **outcomes of care** are the results or consequences to the patient of health care systems, settings, and processes and include measures of morbidity; mortality; social, psychological, and physical functioning; satisfaction with care; and quality of life.

Example 2.8 gives illustrative standards for the evaluation question, "Has the Obstetrical Access and Utilization Initiative improved access to care for high-risk women?

Example 2.8: Structure, Process, and Outcome Standards for an Evaluation Question About Access to Prenatal Care

Structure standard. All waiting rooms will have special play areas for patients' children.

Process standard. All physicians will justify and apply the guidelines prepared by the College of Obstetrics and Gynecology for the number and timing of prenatal care visits to all women.

Outcome standard. Significantly fewer low birth weight babies will be born in the experimental group than in the control group.

Standards must be purposeful; arbitrary standards may doom the program. Suppose the Obstetrical Access and Utilization Initiative aimed to reduce the no-show rate for obstetrical clinic appointments from 30% to 20%. If the rate decreased by only 5%, rather than 10%, would the program be a failure? What about 7%? The answer should be justified by data from other evaluations, the views and ideals of experts, and statistical comparisons.

In addition to being meaningful, standards of effectiveness should be realistic and measurable. Consider the following evaluation question and standard.

Evaluation question: How do students in our medical center compare with students in other medical centers in their knowledge of the content of appropriate prenatal care for high-risk women?

Standard: A statistically significant difference in knowledge will be obtained, favoring our institution.

Unless the evaluation has access to students in other medical centers and can test or observe them in the time allotted for the evaluation, then this standard, although perhaps desirable, is unrealistic and cannot be used.

How to Set Standards

Standards for program evaluations can come from several sources: experts, historical data, comparisons with other groups and comparisons over time, "norms," and epidemiological data.

USING EXPERTS

Experts can assist the evaluator in setting standards. Experts are any individuals or representatives of professional and consumer groups who are likely to use the results of an evaluation.

A variety of techniques is available for structuring group meetings to promote agreement among experts. These usually require the selection of a representative group of experts and the use of structured meetings. For example, if an evaluator is concerned with setting standards for a program to improve the quality of instruction in health policy and health services research, then experts in those fields, experts in education, and the consumers of health services research and policy (such as representatives from the public) will be appropriate advisers.

Expert panels have been used extensively in health and medicine. For example, since 1977, the National Institutes of Health has used consensus development conferences to help resolve issues related to the knowledge and use of medical technology such as intraocular lens implantation and the care of patients with conditions such as depression, sleep disorders, traveler's diarrhea, and breast cancer. Since the late 1980s and early 1990s, a number of organizations like the American College of Physicians and the Agency for Health Care Policy and Research have been bringing experts together to come up with "guidelines" for practice for common problems such as pain, high blood pressure, and depression.

The main purpose of coming to "consensus" is to define levels of agreement on controversial subjects and unresolved issues. These methods are therefore extremely germane to setting standards to judge the effectiveness of new programs for which no comparison group data are available. True consensus methods, however, are often difficult to implement because they typically require extensive reviews of the literature on the topic under discussion as well as highly structured methods.

Expert panels have proven to be effective in setting standards of performance, as illustrated in Example 2.9.

Example 2.9: Using Experts to Set Standards

Sixteen U.S. teaching hospitals participated in a 4-year evaluation of a program to improve outpatient care in their group practices. Among the study's major goals were improvements in amount of faculty involvement in the practices, in staff productivity, and in access to care for patients. The evaluators and representatives from each of the 16 hospitals used standards for care set by the Institute of Medicine as a basis for setting standards of program effectiveness before the start of the study. After 2 years, the evaluators presented interim data on performance and brought the 16 practices together to come to consensus on standards for the final 2 years of the study. To guide the process, the evaluators prepared this form:

Varia-ble	Current Standard	Definitions	Interim Results	Question	Suggestion	Your Decision
Wait-ing Time	90% of patients should be seen within 30 minutes	Waiting time is time between scheduled appointment and when first seen by primary provider	70% of patients were seen within 30 minutes	Is 90% reason-able?	90%	___%
	Compared to national data bases, program patients should not have unduly long waiting times		Waiting times = 24.3 minutes. National data = 37.3 minutes for doctor's office or private clinic.	Should national data be used as standard?	Yes	_Yes _No

Figure 2.2. Selected Portions of a Form Used in Setting Standards of Effectiveness

It is interesting to note that a survey of participants in the standard-setting process found that they did not use the interim data to make their choices: No association was found between how well a medical center had previously performed with respect to each of 36 selected standards and the choice of a performance level for the remaining 2 years of the evaluation. Interviews with the medical centers revealed that the standards that were selected came from informed estimates of what performance might yet become and from the medical centers' ideals; the interim data were considered to be merely suggestive.

A number of methods relying on panels of experts have been used to promote understanding of issues, topics, and standards for program evaluation, but the most productive have depended upon a few simple practices, as discussed in the guidelines shown on pages 32-33.

USING HISTORICAL DATA OR PAST PERFORMANCE

The past performance of a group (or a similar group) is sometimes used as a standard against which to investigate a program's merits. This approach to standard setting has some problems associated with it, however. History often does not repeat itself exactly. As a result, any standards based on previous performance, even with very similar programs and participants, may turn out to be inappropriate. Sometimes the new standards will be too low; at other times, they may be too high.

Guidelines for Expert Panels

1. The evaluation questions must be clearly specified. If they are not, the experts may help in clarification and in specification. Here are examples:

Not quite ready for standard setting: Was the program effective with high-risk women?

More amenable to standard setting: Did the program improve the proportion of low-weight births among low-income women?

Standard: Significantly fewer low-weight births are found in the experimental versus the control group.

2. Data should be provided to assist the experts. These data can be about the participants in the experimental program, the intervention itself, and the costs and benefits of participation. The data can come from the published literature, from ongoing research, or from financial and statistical records. For example, in an evaluation of a program to improve birth weight among low-income women, experts might make use of information about the extent of the problem in the country. They might also want to know how prevalent low birth weight is among poor women, and if other interventions have been used effectively, what their costs were.

3. The experts should qualify for selection because they are knowledgeable, influential, or will use the findings. The number of experts to choose is necessarily dependent upon the evaluation's resources and the evaluator's skill in coordinating groups. Example 2.10 gives two illustrations of the choice of experts.

USING COMPARISONS

Comparative standards are among the most convincing. Comparisons can be made of one group's performance over time, among several groups' performance at one time, or among several groups' performance over time. It is sometimes difficult, however, to constitute similar comparison groups,

Guidelines *(Continued)*

Example 2.10: Choosing Experts to Set Evaluation Standards

- The New Dental Clinic aimed to improve patient satisfaction. A meeting was held in which three patient representatives, a nurse, a physician, and a technician defined the "satisfied patient" and decided on how much time to allow the clinic to produce satisfied patients.

- The primary goals of the Adolescent Outreach Program are to teach teens about preventive health and to make sure that all needed health care services (such as vision screening and immunizations) are provided. A group of teens participated in a teleconference to help the program developers and evaluators decide on the best ways to teach teens and to set standards of learning achievement. Also, physicians, nurses, teachers, and parents participated in a conference to determine the types of services that should be provided and the numbers of teens that should receive them.

4. *The process should be carefully structured and skillfully led.* A major purpose is to come to agreement on the criteria for appraising a program's performance. To facilitate agreement, and distinguish the panel process from an open-ended committee meeting, an agenda should be prepared in advance, along with all materials (such as literature reviews and other presentations of data). When possible, it helps to focus the panel on particular tasks such as asking them to review a specific set of data and to rate the extent to which it applies to the current program. For example, the experts can be given data on past performance (e.g., 10 of 16 hospitals had continuous quality improvement systems for monitoring the quality of inpatient care) and asked to rate the extent to which that standard should still apply (e.g., strongly agree, agree, disagree, strongly disagree).

engage their cooperation, and also have a period of time available that is of sufficient duration for observing differences, if any truly exist. It is extremely important to note that, just because an evaluation finds that one group is different than the other, and the difference favors the new program, one cannot automatically assume an effective program is at work. At least three questions must be asked before any such judgment is possible:

1. Were the groups comparable to begin with? (After all, by coincidence, one group might be smarter, healthier, more compliant, and so on.)
2. Is the magnitude of the difference large enough to be meaningful? With very large samples, small differences (in scores on a standardized test of achievement, for example) can be statistically, but not practically, significant.
3. Are the final levels of performance meaningful? For example, if you find significant changes in attitudes over time, you must also consider whether the extent of change is large enough to have practical implications; even large changes may still be insufficient.

USING NORMS OR EPIDEMIOLOGICAL DATA

Norms and epidemiological data can serve as standards. If you know the current percentage of low-weight births in this state, for example, then you can use that percentage as a gauge for evaluating the effectiveness of a new statewide program that aims to lower the rate. Example 2.11 shows the use of norms as a standard in program evaluation:

Example 2.11: Using Norms as Standards in Program Evaluation

The Obstetrical Access and Utilization Initiative serves high-risk women and aims to avoid the birth of babies weighing less than 2,500 grams (5.5 pounds). One evaluation question asks, "Is the birth of low-weight babies prevented?"

In the state, 6.1% of babies are low birth weight, but this percentage includes babies born to women with low or medium risks. The standard used as evidence that low birth weight is prevented is as follows: "No more than 6.1% of babies will be born weighing less than 5.5 pounds."

When using norms or epidemiological data as comparisons, you must make certain that they are truly applicable. The only data available to you may have been collected at other times and under different circumstances and simply may not apply. For example, data gleaned from an evaluation conducted with men may not apply to women; with older men, the findings may not apply to younger men; and with hospitalized patients, the findings may not apply to people in the community.

Evaluation Questions and Standards: Establishing a Healthy Relationship

An evaluation question may have just one standard, or it may have several standards associated with it:

Question: Did nurses learn to reliably abstract medical records?

Standard 1: 80% of all nurses learn to reliably abstract medical records.

Standard 2: A statistically significant difference in learning is observed between nurses at Medical Center A and those in Medical Center B. Nurses in Medical Center A have participated in a new program, and the difference is in their favor.

The purpose of the two standards in this example is based on the view that, if 80% of nurses at Medical Center A are found able to reliably abstract medical records, you cannot really attribute this positive result to a program unless you have access to the abstractions of nurses who were not in a program. After all, nearly all nurses might know from the start how to abstract medical records. So why not just rely on the second standard? Because differences alone, no matter how great, may not be enough.

Suppose that nurses' learning in Medical Center A was actually significantly higher than that in Medical Center B. If the level of both groups was low (say, average scores of 50% in the new program group and 20% in the comparison), then the difference, although statistically meaningful, might not be educationally or clinically meaningful, and thus it has little practical merit. You can conclude, for example, that, even though the program successfully elevated performance, the amount of improvement was insufficient, and so the program just did not make it.

When to Set Standards

Standards should be in place before continuing with the evaluation's design and analysis. Consider this:

EXAMPLE 1

Program goal: To teach nurses to reliably abstract medical records

Evaluation question: Have nurses learned to reliably abstract medical records?

Standard: 90% of all nurses learn to reliably abstract medical records

Program effects on: Nurses

Effects measured by: Reliable abstraction

Design: A survey of nurses' abstractions

Data collection: A test of nurses' ability to abstract medical records

Statistical analysis: Compute the percentage of nurses who reliably abstract medical records

EXAMPLE 2

Program goal: To teach nurses to reliably abstract medical records

Evaluation question: Have nurses learned to reliably abstract medical records?

Standard: A statistically significant difference in learning is observed between nurses in Medical Centers A and B. Nurses in Medical Center A have participated in a new program, and the difference is in their favor.

Program effects on: Nurses in Medical Center A

Effects measured by: Reliable abstraction

Design: A comparison of two groups of nurses

Data collection: A test of nurses' ability to abstract medical records

Statistical analysis: A *t*-test to compare average abstraction scores between Medical Centers A and B

The evaluation questions and standards prescribe the evaluation's design, data collection, and analysis. They do this because they contain the independent and dependent variables upon which the evaluation's design, measurement, and analysis are subsequently based.

Independent variables are sometimes called "explanatory" or "predictor variables." Because they are present before the start of the program or are independent of it, evaluators use them to "explain" or "predict" outcomes. In the example above, reliable abstraction of medical records (the outcome) is to be explained by nurses' participation in a new program (the independent variable). In evaluations, the independent variables often are the program (experimental and control), demographic features of the participants (such as gender, income, education, experience), and health characteristics (such as functional status and physical, mental, and social health).

Dependent variables, also termed "outcome variables," are the factors the evaluator expects to measure. In program evaluations, these include health status, functional status, knowledge, skills, attitudes, behavior, costs, and efficiency.

The evaluation questions and standards necessarily contain the independent and dependent variables: those on whom the program is to have an effect and measures of those effects, as illustrated in Example 2.12:

Example 2.12: Questions, Standards, and Independent and Dependent Variables

Program goal: To teach nurses to reliably abstract medical records

Evaluation question: Have nurses learned to reliably abstract medical records?

Standard: A statistically significant difference in learning is observed between nurses in Medical Centers A and B. Nurses in Medical Center A have par-

ticipated in a new program, and the difference is in their favor.

Program effects explained by (independent variable): Participation versus no participation in a new program

Effects measured by this outcome (dependent variable): Reliable abstraction

The QSV Report:
Questions, Standards, Variables

The relationship among questions, standards, and variables can be depicted in the Evaluation Questions, Standards, and Variables Reporting Form, Figure 2.3. This report is useful for planning the evaluation and accounting for its methods. The form is a chart with four columns. The first contains the evaluation questions; the second, the standards associated with each question; the third, the independent variables; and the fourth, the dependent variables.

The QSV Report is illustrated for an 18-month program combining diet and exercise to improve health status and quality of life for persons 75 years of age or older who are living at home. Participants will be randomly assigned to the experimental or control groups according to the street on which they live. Participants in the evaluation who need medical services can choose one of two clinics offering differing models of delivering care, one that is primarily staffed by physicians and one that is primarily staffed by nurses. The evaluators will be investigating whether any differences after program participation exist for men and women and the role of patient mix in those differences. **Patient mix** refers to those characteristics of patients that might affect outcomes and includes sociodemographic characteristics, functional status scores, and presence of chronic disorders such as diabetes and hypertension. The evaluators will also be analyzing the cost-effectiveness of the two models of health care delivery.

Evaluation Questions	Standards	Independent or Explanatory Variables	Dependent or Outcome Variables
To what extent has quality of life improved?	A statistically and practically significant improvement in quality of life over a 1-year period A statistically and p.actically significant improvement in quality of life between participants and nonparticipants	Gender, group participation (experimental and control participants), patient mix (sociodemographic characteristics, functional status scores, presence or absence of chronic disorders such as diabetes and hypertension)	Quality of life includes social contacts and support, financial support, perceptions of well-being
To what extent has health status improved?	A statistically and practically significant improvement in quality of life over a 1-year period A statistically and practically significant improvement in quality of life between participants and nonparticipants	Gender, group participation (experimental and control participants), patient mix of measures (sociodemographic characteristics; functional status scores, presence or absence of chronic disorders such as diabetes and hypertension)	Health status includes functional status and perceptions of general health and physical functioning; measures of complications from illness (for diabetes would include cardiac, renal, ophthalmologic, or foot; for hypertension would include blood pressure control)
What is the relationship between cost and effectiveness of two clinic-staffing models: primarily physicians and primarily nurses?	Effectiveness will be demonstrated by lower cost per visit and satisfactory health status and quality of life	Two models of care (primarily physician- and primarily nurse-based)	Quality of life, health status, costs of personnel, hours delivering care, number of appointments made and kept

Figure 2.3. The Questions, Standards, and Variables (QSV) Reporting Form

As you can see, the chart extracts the questions, standards, and variables from the description of the evaluation of the diet and exercise program for persons over 75 years of age. This evaluation has three questions about the program's influence on quality-of-life and health status and the cost-effectiveness of two methods for staffing clinics. Each of the three questions has one or more standards associated with it. The independent variables for the questions about quality-of-life and health status are gender, group participation, and patient mix; each term, such as *patient mix,* is explained. The dependent variables are also explained in the QSV. For example, quality of life is explained as including social contacts and support, financial support, and perceptions of well-being.

SUMMARY AND TRANSITION TO THE NEXT CHAPTER ON EVALUATION RESEARCH DESIGN

Evaluations are conducted to determine if a program is meritorious. Was it worth the costs, or might a more efficient program accomplish even more? Evaluation questions focus the evaluation. They may be about the program's environment; the extent to which program goals and objectives have been met; the degree, duration, and distribution of benefits and effects; and the implementation and effectiveness of different program activities and management strategies.

Program evaluations are concerned with providing convincing evidence that a program is effective. The standards are the specific criteria according to which effectiveness is established. Standards should be set in advance of any evaluation activities because they prescribe the evaluation's design, data collection, and analysis. One question may have more than one standard associated with it. Standards come from experts, the literature, past performance, epidemiological data, and statistical comparisons.

The next chapter will tell you how to design an evaluation so that any changes in health, health practices, education, and attitudes can be linked to an experimental program and not to other competing events. For example, suppose you were evaluating a health education program aiming to encourage men and women over 50 to get a colonoscopy—a rather uncomfortable procedure that has been shown to protect against colon cancer. You might erroneously conclude that your program is effective if you observed a significant increase in colonoscopies among participants in your program, unless your evaluation's design was sufficiently sophisticated to distinguish between the effects of the health education program and other sources of education such as television and newspapers. The next chapter will discuss the most commonly used evaluation research designs.

EXERCISE: EVALUATION QUESTIONS AND STANDARDS

Directions

1. Read the example below and, using only the information offered, list the evaluation questions.

> The University Medical Center is concerned with continuously auditing its transfusion practices to ensure the safety of the blood supply. Accordingly, a Committee on Blood Derivatives has been formed to establish guidelines for transfusing red blood cells, fresh frozen plasma, platelets, and cryoprecipitated AHF. An education program is offered to all interested physicians and nurses to teach them about the guidelines, assist in ensuring appropriate transfusion practices, and, in general, improve the quality of care at the institution. A 2-year evaluation is conducted. Among the medical center's concerns is that all physicians use the guidelines.

2. Read the example below and state the evaluation questions and associated standards as well as the independent and dependent variables.

> The Infectious Disease Center is concerned that its nonphysician staff acquire knowledge regarding some of the ethical issues pertaining to the care of patients with infectious diseases including hepatitis and tuberculosis. These specifically include issues pertaining to patient privacy. The center's director is working with the bioethics committee and the division of medical education to develop a program for nonphysicians. The plan is to institute the program and monitor its effects on staff each year for 5 years.

Suggested Readings

Adams, M. E., McCall, N. T., Gray, D. T., et al. (1992). Economic analysis in randomized control trials. *Medical Care, 30,* 231-243.

This is a report of a study of the prevalence and completeness of economic analyses in randomized controlled trials. The criteria for prevalence and completeness are of interest to health program evaluators who are concerned with answering questions about cost-effectiveness.

The following are other references showing the use of questions about costs.

Foote, A., & Erfut, J. C. (1991). The benefit-to-cost ratio of work-site blood pressure control problems. *Journal of the American Medical Association, 265,* 1283-1286.

Gravely, E., & Littlefield, J. H. (1992). A cost-effectiveness analysis of three staffing models for the delivery of low-risk prenatal care. *American Journal of Public Health, 82,* 180-184.

Kosecoff, J., Brook, R. H., Fink, A., et al. (1987). Providing primary care in university hospitals: Efficiency and cost. *Annals of Internal Medicine, 107,* 399-405.

Donabedian, A. (1980). *Explorations in quality assessment and monitoring* (Vol. 1). Ann Arbor, MI: Health Administration Press.

Donabedian, A. (1982). *The definition of quality and approaches to its assessment* (Vol. 2). Ann Arbor, MI: Health Administration Press.

Donabedian, A. (1983). *The criteria and standards of monitoring* (Vol. 3). Ann Arbor, MI: Health Administration Press.

These volumes contain the classic definitions and explanations of how to assess quality of care in terms of its structure, process, and outcome.

Fink, A., Kosecoff, J., & Brook, R. H. (1986). Setting standards of performance for program evaluations: The case of the teaching hospital general medicine group practice program. *Evaluation and Program Planning, 9,* 143-151.

Describes the methods and usefulness of setting standards in a national study to improve the quality of care and education for health care practitioners.

Purpose of This Chapter

An evaluation design is a structure that is created especially to produce an unbiased appraisal of a program's merits. The structure is built on the independent variables and the frequency and timing of measurement. This chapter discusses the relationships between evaluation designs and the evaluation questions and standards. It also explains the uses and limitations of experimental and observational evaluation designs. The role of the Evaluation Design Chart in establishing the logical connections between the purposes and methods of the evaluation is also discussed.

3 Designing Program Evaluations

Evaluation Design: Creating the Structure

An evaluation design is a structure created especially to appraise a program's effectiveness objectively and without bias. Consider Examples 3.1, 3.2, and 3.3, which follow.

Example 3.1: Evaluation Design: The Same Group Is Measured over Time

Narrative

A new Spanish-language health education program for fifth graders is being evaluated in the district's 12 elementary schools. If effective, it will replace the traditional program. A key evaluation question is whether participating students' knowledge improves. To be eligible for participation, students must read in Spanish at the fifth-grade level or better. Improvement is to be analyzed statistically. Students will be tested within 1 month of the beginning of the program and after 1 year to determine how much is learned.

Abstract

Program: A new fifth-grade Spanish-language health education program

Evaluation question: Does students' knowledge improve?

Standard: Statistically significant improvement over time

Independent variable: Students in the new program

Eligibility for evaluation: All 12 elementary schools are eligible

Eligibility for the program: Students must read at the fifth-grade level or better in Spanish

Measurement: A test of students' knowledge within 1 month of the beginning of the experimental program, and a test of the same students' knowledge 1 year after completion of the program

---

In Example 3.1, all schools and eligible students will participate in the evaluation; they will be measured before and after participation. In Example 3.2, six schools will be selected at random to participate in the evaluation, and

---

Example 3.2: Evaluation Design with Random Selection and Measurement over Time

Narrative

A new Spanish-language health education program for fifth graders is being evaluated in six of the district's twelve elementary schools. The six will be selected at random. If effective, the program will be introduced throughout the district's twelve elementary schools. A key evaluation question is whether students' knowledge improves. To participate, students must read in Spanish at the fifth-grade level or better. Improvement is to be analyzed statistically. Students will be tested within 1 month of the beginning of the program and after 1 year to determine how much is learned.

Abstract

Program: A new fifth-grade Spanish-language health education program

Evaluation question: Does students' knowledge improve?

Independent variable: Students in six elementary schools participating in a new program

Standard: Statistically significant improvement over time

Eligibility for the evaluation: Six of twelve elementary schools in the district

Selection for the evaluation: Six schools will be selected at random

Eligibility for the program: Students who read at the fifth-grade level or better in Spanish

Measurement: A test of students' knowledge within 1 month of the beginning of the experimental program, and a test of students' knowledge 1 year after completion of the program

Example 3.3: Evaluation Design with Random Selection and Randomly Assigned Groups Measured over Time

Narrative

A new Spanish-language health education program for fifth graders is being evaluated in six elementary schools. If effective, it will be introduced throughout the district's twelve elementary schools. The six participating schools will be chosen at random. Of the six, three will be randomly assigned to continue with their regular health education program, and students in the other three will participate in the new one. A key evaluation question is whether students' knowledge improves. Improvement is to be analyzed statistically. To participate, students have to read in Spanish at the fifth-grade level or better. Students will be tested within 1 month of the beginning of the program and after 1 year to determine how much is learned.

Abstract

Program: A new fifth-grade Spanish-language health education program

Evaluation question: Does students' knowledge improve?

Independent variable: Students in an experimental and in a control program

Standard: Statistically significant improvement over time

Eligibility for the evaluation: Six of nine elementary schools in the district

Selection for the evaluation: Six schools will be selected at random

Eligibility for the program: Students who read at the fifth-grade level or better in Spanish

Assignment to groups: Three schools will be assigned at random to the experimental program; the students in the other three will be assigned to continue with the traditional district-approved health education program

Measurement: A test of students' knowledge within 1 month of the beginning of the program, and a test of students' knowledge 1 year after completion of the program

eligible students will be tested before and after participation. In Example 3.3, three of the schools will be assigned at random into the new or experimental program; eligible students in the other three schools will receive the regular program. Students in the third example will also be measured twice: before and after the intervention.

These three examples are illustrative of three basic program evaluation designs: experimental evaluation designs with nonrandom selection into the evaluation and relying on one group to act as a control or comparison for itself (using a premeasure and a postmeasure); experimental evaluation designs with random selection into the evaluation and relying on one group to act as a control or comparison for itself (using a premeasure and a postmeasure); and experimental evaluation designs with random selection into the evaluation and random assignment into experimental and control groups and a premeasure and postmeasure.

Before designing an evaluation, at least six questions should be answered. The answers to the questions are given below and are followed with answers from the examples taken from the new Spanish-language health education program.

QUESTIONS TO ASK WHEN DESIGNING EVALUATIONS

1. What are the evaluation questions and standards?
2. What are the independent variables?
3. What are the inclusion and exclusion criteria?
4. Will a control group be included?
   a. If yes, what are the characteristics of the control group?
5. When will measures be taken?
6. How often will measures be taken?

Selecting an Evaluation Design: Dealing With Six Questions

1. WHAT ARE THE EVALUATION QUESTIONS AND STANDARDS?

A first step in the selection of any evaluation design is to turn to the evaluation questions and their associated standards. The standard is the guide to a *minimum* design. If the standard calls for changes over time, for example, you know that a design is needed in which two measurements are taken. This is the case for all three evaluation examples given above. In Example 3.3, however, the evaluation also combines the two measurements with two groups. The addition of a comparison group to a design always strengthens it. Suppose, for example, an evaluation found that fifth graders improved in their knowledge of preventive health care after their participation in an experimental program. Unless the evaluator can demonstrate that fifth graders in comparable programs do not also improve, claims that the new program is effective can be challenged. Fifth graders can improve in their knowledge for several reasons—among them, ordinary intellectual maturation.

2. WHAT ARE THE INDEPENDENT VARIABLES?

Independent variables are also called "explanatory" or "predictor variables" because they are used to explain or predict the program's outcomes (the dependent variables). They are independent of the program and are part of the evaluation's structure or design.

In evaluations, the independent variables are often group participation (experimental group and control groups) and the participants' social and health status. The evaluator uses these variables in hypothesizing or predicting the outcomes (dependent variables) of program participation. Consider the relationship among the following evaluation questions, standards, independent variables, and outcomes.

Relationship Among Evaluation Questions, Standards, Independent Variables, and Outcomes

A. Evaluation question: How do participants in the experimental and control groups compare in their social activity?

Standard: A statistically significant difference in social activity, favoring the experimental group.

Independent variable: Group participation (in the experimental or in the control group)

Outcome (dependent variable): Social activity

Evaluator's prediction: Participation in the experimental program will be associated with increased and higher quality social activity than participation in the control program.

B. Evaluation question: How do low-income women in the new prenatal care program compare with low-income women in the traditional program in their attendance at childbirth and parenting classes?

Standard: A statistically significant difference between the new and traditional program in attendance, favoring the new program

Independent variable: Group participation (in the new prenatal care program or in the traditional program)

Outcome (dependent variable): Attendance at childbirth and parenting classes

Evaluator's prediction: Participation in the new program will be associated with increased attendance at childbirth and parenting classes.

Once the evaluator has the questions, standards, independent variables, and outcomes, the design comes next.

Evaluation Question, Standards, Independent Variables, Outcomes, and Design

Evaluation question: To what extent has quality of life improved after participation in the Healthy Adult Program?

Standard: A statistically and practically significant improvement in quality of life between male and female participants and nonparticipants whose problems vary in complexity

Independent variables: Group participation, gender, problem mix (a combination of economic characteristics and health and functional status)

Outcome (dependent variable): Quality of life

Design:

	Experimental	Control
Males		
Very complex problems		
Average complexity		
Not very complex problems		
Females		
Very complex problems		
Average complexity		
Not very complex problems		

The independent variables frame the design. In some cases, the frame is relatively easy to create because the categories are self-evident as they are for gender (male and female) and group participation (experimental and control). But, for other independent variables like patient mix, age, health status, and so on, deciding on categories becomes more complicated. In this example, "patient mix," which refers to a combination of economic, health, and functional differences, was divided into three categories: very complex, average, and not very complex. But other categories might have been chosen to describe patient mix. For example, the three components of patient mix might have been treated separately, with patients assigned to groups depending upon their scores on measures of health, functioning, and income. The choice of categories depends on what the literature says (Are data available that suggest the most accurate way to define problem mix?) and resources (How many groups can you afford to include in the evaluation?).

3. WHAT ARE THE INCLUSION AND EXCLUSION CRITERIA?

These criteria (sometimes called "eligibility criteria") separate those who are eligible for participation in the evaluation from those who are not and are the foundation for inferring conclusions about the groups who are most likely to benefit from participation. For example, assume that an evaluation of a program to improve preventive personal health practices includes only women under 50 years of age with diabetes. Suppose also that the evaluation cannot afford to provide transportation to the program's location for women who do not have their own transportation, and so these women are excluded. If the program is effective, the nature of the exclusion criteria will necessarily limit the program's applicability to women under 50 years with diabetes who have access to transportation.

Criteria for inclusion into an evaluation sometimes come from primarily practical considerations. These consist of parameters such as geographic and temporal proximity and demographic and health characteristics. Consider the illustrative inclusion criteria in Example 3.4:

Example 3.4: Illustrative Inclusion or Eligibility Criteria

Inclusion Criteria

- Schools offering health education to fifth graders
- Women seen in the clinic during the past 2 years

- Health centers serving 50 or more new clients each week
- Health centers serving 50 or more new female clients each week

---

Evaluations sometimes have exclusion criteria. These are special criteria that apply to potential participants whose inclusion is likely to impair the actual functioning of the evaluation or skew its data. Consider these sample exclusion criteria in Example 3.5:

Example 3.5: Illustrative Exclusion Criteria

Exclusion Criteria

- Schools whose fifth-grade health education program meets less than once a week
- Articles published before 1990

- People with major mental disorders such as schizophrenia who are unlikely to comply with program rules

---

In addition to practical considerations, eligibility criteria come from the evaluation questions, as illustrated in Example 3.6:

Example 3.6: Inclusion and Exclusion Criteria: The Evaluation Questions

1. Evaluation question: Has access to prenatal care for high-risk pregnant women improved?

Ask: Which high-risk groups must be included for this program to receive a fair trial? To which high-risk groups are the findings to be applied? Where and when can I obtain these women for participation?

Inclusion Criteria:

- Must live within 10 miles of the clinic
- Teenage mothers with at least one other child living at home
- Women between 30 and 40 years of age who are eligible for Medicaid

Exclusion Criteria:

- Women with private health insurance
- Women between 20 and 29 years of age

2. Evaluation question: Have students improved their knowledge of health?

Ask: What are the characteristics of students that must be included for this program to receive a fair trial? To which groups of students should the findings be applicable? Where and when can I get these students to participate?

Inclusion Criteria:

- Must be in one of the district's elementary schools
- Students whose reading abilities in Spanish are at the fifth-grade level or better

Exclusion Criteria:

- Students whose teachers have less than 1 year's experience teaching health education
- Students with a grade point average of less than 3.0
- Students who were absent in the past year an average of 5 or more days each month

---

4. WILL A CONTROL GROUP BE INCLUDED?

The term "group" refers to the institutions and individuals who participate in the evaluation, regardless of whether or not they receive the experimental intervention. A typical evaluation design consists of an experimental and a control group. The experimental group is given the new program, and the control receives some other program. This is a fundamental design, and it can be represented like this:

Experimental Group	Control Group

Figure 3.1. A Basic Evaluation Design: The Experimental and Control Groups Compared

Some evaluations have more than one experimental group and also more than one control. For example, suppose a hypothetical new school-based preventive health care program for fifth graders wants to compare two different styles of instruction: computer-assisted (Program A) and small group discussion (Program B). Suppose also that the evaluator proposes two control groups: teacher-directed lecture and discussion (Control 1) and self-instructional learning modules (Control 2). The design for this evaluation is depicted in Figure 3.2.

	Experimental Program A: Computer-Assisted Instruction	Experimental Program B: Small Group Discussion
Control Program 1: Teacher Directed		
Control Program 2: Self-Instructional Modules		

Figure 3.2. An Evaluation Design for a Program Comparing Instructional Methods: Two Experimental and Two Control Groups

This design enables the evaluator to compare the achievement of learning objectives by students in the following situations:

- ◆ Experimental Programs A versus B
- ◆ Control Programs 1 and 2
- ◆ Experimental Program A and Controls 1 and 2
- ◆ Experimental Program B and Controls 1 and 2

In an evaluation, what program should the control group receive? This very important question often is not given the attention it deserves. Frequently, the control program consists of the usual services or no services at all. A control group must start out to be demonstrably like the experimental group in its composition (health status, knowledge, attitudes, demographic characteristics) but definably and measurably unlike it in its program. Programs can differ in their philosophies, objectives, methods, settings, duration, management, and resources.

5. WHEN WILL MEASURES TAKE PLACE?

In evaluations, measures can be made before and after the program, during the program, or just after. Premeasures can serve many important evaluation purposes, for example, to select groups to participate in the evaluation and program, check the need for the program, ensure comparability of groups, and provide a basis for calculating change or improvement. The merit of using premeasures can be compromised, however, if they are not demonstrably similar to the postmeasures, if they are administered very close in time to the postmeasure (because people may simply repeat their responses from the premeasure), and if they influence program participants to behave or perform in special ways (by focusing people's attention on program content). Figure 3.3 gives illustrative uses of premeasures and postmeasures.

Measure	Uses	Comments
Premeasure to select groups	Students were tested for their ability to read Spanish to identify those with reading levels at fifth grade or better. A financial analysis was conducted to identify women eligible for welfare assistance.	Data such as these (reading level and financial status) are often available from records. Using existing data can save time.
Premeasure to check the need for the program	A pretest of students' knowledge revealed that they already knew a substantial portion of the information to be imparted in the new curriculum. A financial analysis revealed that more women are eligible than the original estimates for the new program suggested.	This information can be used to revise the program or the evaluation questions and standards.
Premeasure to ensure comparability of groups	Schools A, B, and C, who volunteered for the program, were found to have more experienced health education teachers than Control Schools X, Y, and Z. No differences were found in the ages, marital status, health status, or income of women in the volunteer experimental and control groups.	Differences between or among groups before the start of the program can easily bias the results. Determining the nature and extent of potential "contaminants" is essential in program evaluation.

Figure 3.3. Illustrative Uses of Premeasures and Postmeasures

Measure	Uses	Comments
Premeasure to provide a basis for measuring change or improvement	Students in the experimental group gained significantly more knowledge than did a control group. Women in the experimental group did not enter care earlier than women in the control.	Premeasures provide a baseline against which to measure progress for single groups ("self controls") and for multiple groups.
Postmeasure to appraise benefit, outcome, impact, cost	Average scores on a test were compared between the experimental and control groups after participation in a health education program. The numbers of women entering prenatal care before the third trimester are compared after half participated in a program to improve access to care.	Postmeasures provide evidence of a program's merits. They include achievement tests; surveys (interviews, telephone, self-administered questionnaires); observations; and record reviews.

Figure 3.3. (Continued)

6. HOW OFTEN WILL MEASURES TAKE PLACE?

The frequency of measures should be dependent upon how much time is needed for the program's effects to occur, the duration of the program and the evaluation, and the resources available for measurement. The time needed to observe and be able to measure a program's hoped-for effects varies according to the characteristics of the expected outcomes, impact, and costs. For example, assessing students at the end of a year to determine the effects of a program to teach specific health education content to fifth graders is probably reasonable. Assessing changes in health habits and associated costs at the end of 1 year would be foolhardy, however, because these changes usually take longer than 1 year to observe. To identify the expected amount of time to uncover changes in health habits, practices, and costs, a literature review or survey of experts is often indicated. Remember, the longer the period needed for measurement and observation, the more opportunity external effects (such as changes in the health care reimbursement system, for example, or changes due to children's physical and social maturation) will have to interact with and "confound" the results.

Yearly measurement to search for long-term changes may be indicated, but programs and their evaluations rarely last more than 3 to 5 years. To ensure the possibility of continuous evaluation, a data collection system can be created and continuously updated.

Designs for Program Evaluation

Evaluations aim to be prospective investigations of a program's characteristics and effectiveness. In a prospective investigation, data are collected for the specific purposes of the evaluation, commencing with the start of the evaluation. To demonstrate this point, consider the following illustrations in Example 3.7.

Example 3.7: Evaluations Are Prospective

Prospective Evaluation A: An evaluation asked if fifth graders' knowledge improved after their participation in a health education program. A test was given to the students 1 month before the program started and 1 year after their participation. Performance was compared over time.

Retrospective Study B: For the past 5 years, the school district has administered an achievement test to all fifth graders to find out about their knowledge of preventive health care. At the end of the fifth year, test records were reviewed to identify high and low scorers. The two groups were compared to determine if a relationship existed between participation in a new program and scores.

Prospective Evaluation C: Does participation in the Obstetrical Access and Utilization Project improve birth outcomes for high-risk women? Data were collected on mothers from the time of their entry into the project and for 6 months after the birth of their babies. An evaluation was conducted that compared babies born to participating and nonparticipating mothers in terms of their mortality, morbidity, birth weight, and gestational age.

Retrospective Study D: Does participation in the Obstetrical Access and Utilization Project improve birth outcomes for high-risk women? After 3 years of the project's installation, birth and death certificates were studied. Among the findings was that significantly fewer very low birth-weight babies were born to women in the project.

The best program evaluations are prospective because they are amenable to the most "control." Retrospective studies are sometimes called "summative evaluations." These are historical analyses and leave too much to chance to satisfy the demands of a diligent investigation of a program's characteristics and merits.

In example B, for example, assume that all high scorers were found to have participated in the district's new program. Can the evaluator conclude that the program was effective? Perhaps the high scorers were more knowledgeable to begin with. In example C, the positive findings can be a reflection of the characteristics of women who participated in the project rather than a reflection of the effectiveness of the project. (They may have been more educated about prenatal care, more willing to comply with medical and nursing advice, and so on.) Advance control over the contents of the program, over selection and assignment to groups, and over data collection is essential in ensuring the validity of an evaluation's findings.

The following designs have been selected because they are most appropriate for program evaluations. Observational designs are included because they are frequently used in evaluations and have a major role to play in them. Because program evaluations borrow from a number of disciplines, you will find that several terms (such as "true experiment" and "randomized controlled" or "control trial") are sometimes used synonymously by evaluators. These terms are explained as they come up in the text.

A Classification of Program Evaluation Designs

I. Experiments

A. Evaluations with concurrent controls in which participants are randomly assigned to groups. These are called "randomized controlled" or "control trials" or "true experiments."

B. Evaluations with concurrent controls in which participants are not randomly assigned to groups. These are called "nonrandomized controlled trials" or "quasi experiments."

C. Evaluations with self-controls. These require premeasures and postmeasures and are called "longitudinal evaluations" or "before-and-after designs."

D. Evaluations with historical controls: These make use of data collected on participants in other evaluations and research studies.

II. Observational designs

A. Surveys or cross sections
B. Cohorts

III. Combination designs

EXPERIMENTAL EVALUATIONS

*Evaluations With Concurrent Controls
and Random Assignment*

With this evaluation design, a group of potential program participants (e.g., persons over 75 years of age, children in need of polio vaccinations, high-risk men) are identified. They are then assigned at random to the new program or the control. The program is introduced concurrently to both groups, and the two groups are compared on some outcome of interest (e.g., health status). This design is sometimes called a "randomized trial" or a "randomized controlled" or "control trial" or a "true experiment."

In some randomized controlled trials, the participants and investigators do not know which group is the experimental one and which is the control: This is the double-blind experiment. When participants do not know, but investigators do, this is called the blinded trial.

In evaluation studies, it is often logistically or ethically difficult to "blind" participants, and this may introduce bias or error. Another potential source of bias is failure to deliver a uniform program. For example, if two different professors are to teach the same content, their teaching styles may be so different as to "bias" the results.

The randomized controlled trial (RCT) is the fundamental design against which others are judged because causation can be inferred from it. To ensure the generalizability of the results, RCTs of the same intervention should probably be conducted in many places, with a variety of participants, over a number of years.

From the evaluator's perspective, the experimental evaluation with randomly constituted concurrent controls is the ideal, but many factors militate against the use of this design:

- ◆ Evaluators typically lack the resources to conduct a multicenter intervention.
- ◆ Evaluators have difficulty in getting enough participants to constitute groups.
- ◆ Evaluators are not granted the time and money needed to prepare and implement the design.
- ◆ A potential disparity invariably exists between the urgency with which data are needed and the amount of time required to conduct the evaluation.
- ◆ Ethical and other problems arise in randomly assigning and blinding participants and investigators.
- ◆ In very large evaluations, it can be a logistical nightmare to ensure that the program and assessment measures (such as tests and surveys) are being implemented across groups in a uniform way.

Evaluations With Concurrent Controls But No Randomization

Nonrandomized, concurrent controls (quasi-experimental designs) involve the creation of an experimental group and a control group without random assignment. This design is usually easier to implement than a randomized controlled trial. Suppose you were the evaluator of a gerontology fellowship program for physicians. Each year, three physicians in six medical schools will participate. The aim of the 3-year program is to enhance physicians' ability to do health services research in the area of aging. By the end of the third year, 54 fellows in gerontology will have participated. In this example, because the numbers of students and medical schools are relatively small, random assignment really does not make sense.

The use of nonrandomly selected controls in evaluation contains the possibility of bias from additional sources, as illustrated in Example 3.8:

Example 3.8: Biases of Concurrent Controls With Randomization

Membership bias. This bias exists in preexisting groups (e.g., students at this medical center versus students at another) because one or more of the same characteristics that cause people to belong to the groups (e.g., choice of medical centers with differing clinical emphases) are associated with the outcome being evaluated (e.g., attitude toward and knowledge of a particular clinical subject matter).

Nonresponse bias. This bias occurs when participants are invited to volunteer to participate in an evaluation study. For example, suppose faculty are invited to participate in a new geriatrics and gerontology curriculum. Those who accept may be somewhat different than nonaccepters in their willingness to try new educational programs, or they currently may have more time to participate in a new activity, and so on.

Evaluations With Self-Controls

A design with self-controls uses a group of participants to serve as its own comparison. Suppose, for example, an educational evaluator tested nursing students three times: at the beginning of the year to find out how much they knew to begin with, immediately after their participation in a new course to find out how much they learned, and at the end of 2 years to ascertain how much learning they retained. This three-measurement strategy describes an evaluation design using the nursing students as their own control. In the example, the evaluator measures the nurses once before and twice after the intervention (a new course). Designs of this type are also called "before-and-after" or "pretest-posttest" designs.

Evaluations that use self-controls are prone to several biases. These come about when participants are excited about taking part in a new program and especially motivated to do well; participants mature physically, emotionally, and intellectually; or historical events intervene.

For example, suppose the evaluator finds that nursing students in a new course acquire important skills and retain them over time. This result may be due to the new course or to the characteristics of the nursing students who, from the start, may have been motivated to learn and excited by being in an experimental program. Another possibility is that participants may have matured intellectually, and this development rather than the program was responsible for the learning. Also, historical events may have occurred to cloud the effects of the new course. For example, suppose that, during the year, a visiting professor gives several inspiring lectures to the nursing students. The students' performance on subsequent tests may be due as much or more to the lectures as to the program.

The soundness of self-controlled designs is dependent upon the appropriateness of the number and timing of measurements. If the evaluator wanted to check retention of learning, for example, should students be tested once? Twice? At what intervals? A program might be considered ineffective just because data were collected to soon for the hoped-for outcomes to occur.

Evaluations With Historical Controls

Evaluations with historical controls rely on data that are available from some other, recorded source. Historical controls include established norms of height, weight, blood pressure, scores on standardized tests like the SAT and the MCAT, and laboratory values. They may also consist of data from participants in other programs or the same program in another setting. Historical controls are convenient; their main source of bias is the potential lack of comparability between the group on whom the data were originally collected and the group of concern in the evaluation.

OBSERVATIONS

Survey Designs

Evaluators use survey designs to collect baseline information on experimental and control groups, to guide program development, and as a source of data regarding the program and its environment. Survey designs enable the evaluator to present a cross-sectional portrait of one or many groups at one period of time. Example 3.9 illustrates survey designs in program evaluations.

Example 3.9: Survey Designs and Program Evaluation

1. A test of student knowledge of program evaluation principles. The Curriculum Committee wanted information on entering graduate students' knowledge of the methods and uses of program evaluation in improving the public's health. They asked the evaluator to prepare and administer a brief test to all students. The results revealed that 80% could not distinguish survey and experimental evaluation designs, and only 20% could list more than one source for setting standards of program effectiveness. The Curriculum Committee used the findings to develop a course of instruction to provide entering graduate students with skills to conduct and review evaluations.

2. A review of the care of hypertensive patients. A review was conducted of the medical records of 2,500 patients in three medical centers to find out about the management of patients with hypertension. The data are being used to determine whether a program is needed to improve dissemination of practice guidelines for this common medical problem and to determine how that program should be evaluated.

→

Example 3.9 (Continued)

3. A survey of satisfaction with transfusion practices. A survey was conducted of all patients who received transfusions within the past 6 years at the medical center. The findings revealed that nearly 60% of 1,000 respondents were females between 68 and 72 years of age. Nearly half reported that they were familiar with the concept of "autologous" donation. Just over 87% indicated that they were very satisfied with their treatment at the hospital and, if necessary, would not fear another transfusion. Over 50% of 739 family members, however, indicated their concern over the entire process and the safety of transfusions. The findings suggested the need to develop an education program to reassure family members.

Cohort Evaluations

A **cohort** is a group of people who have something in common and who remain part of a group over an extended period of time. In medical research, cohort studies are used to investigate the risk factors for a disease and the disease's cause, incidence, natural history, and prognosis. Cohort studies ask: "What will happen?" They are prospective designs, and the group is followed over time or longitudinally.

In evaluations, the cohort consists of participants in a program who are observed over time to determine the extent to which the program's effects have lasted and how and to what extent program participation influenced the future. For example, a cohort of students in an experimental program to train nurses to administer home health care programs can be monitored over time to find out how many assume leadership positions and the extent to which the knowledge they acquired in the program was sustained and useful. Cohort studies are expensive to conduct because they are long term; they are also subject to biases from selection (those who are chosen and willing to participate in the evaluation may be very different than those who do not participate) and attrition.

COMBINATIONS: THE SOLOMON FOUR-GROUP DESIGN

Evaluation designs can involve two groups who are observed before and after an intervention. A very powerful evaluation design is the Solomon Four-Group, in which participants are randomly assigned to four groups. The design can be depicted as shown in Figure 3.4.

Group 1	Premeasure	Program	Postmeasure
Group 2			Postmeasure
Group 3	Premeasure	Program	Postmeasure
Group 4			Postmeasure

Figure 3.4. The Solomon Four-Group Design

In this example, Groups 1 and 3 participated in a new program, but Groups 2 and 4 did not. Suppose the new program aimed to improve employees' knowledge of health hazards at their place of work. Using the four-group design (and assuming an effective program), the evaluator can expect to find the following:

1. In Group 1, knowledge on the postmeasure should be greater than on the premeasure.
2. More knowledge should be observed in Group 1's postmeasure than in Group 2.
3. Group 3's postmeasure should show more knowledge than Group 2's premeasure.
4. Group 3's postmeasure should show more knowledge than Group 4's postmeasure.

This design is a randomized control trial, and it incorporates self and concurrent controls.

Figure 3.5 is a review of seven major evaluation designs.

Evaluation Design	Benefits	Concerns
Concurrent controls and random assignment (randomized controlled or control trial; true experiment)	If properly conducted, can establish the extent to which a program caused its outcomes.	Difficult to implement logistically and methodologically.
Concurrent controls without randomization (quasi experimental)	Easier to implement than a randomized control trial.	A wide range of potential biases may occur because, without an equal chance of selection, participants in the program may be systematically different than those in the control. Also, the two groups in the evaluation may be systematically different than other, nonparticipating groups.

Figure 3.5. Review of Evaluation Designs: Benefits and Concerns

Evaluation Design	Benefits	Concerns
Self-controls	Relatively easy to implement logistically. Provides data on change and improvement.	Must be certain that measurements are appropriately timed. Without a control group, the evaluator cannot tell if seemingly experimental effects are also present in other groups.
Historical controls	Easy to implement; unobtrusive.	Must make sure that "normative" comparison data are applicable to participants in the evaluation.
Survey designs (cross-sectional)	Provides baseline information on the evaluation's participants and descriptive information on the program and its setting and resources.	Offers a static picture of participants and program at one point in time.
Cohort	Provides longitudinal or follow-up information.	Can be expensive because they are relatively long-term studies. Participants who are available over time may differ in important ways from those who are not.
Solomon Four-Group	Rigorous design that can enable evaluator to infer causation. Guards against the effects of the premeasure on subsequent performance.	Need to have enough participants to constitute four groups. Expensive to implement.

Figure 3.5. (Continued)

Internal and External Validity

The terms **internal validity** and **external validity** are sometimes used in connection with an evaluation's design. A design is internally valid if it enables the evaluator to be confident that a program is effective in a specific experimental instance. If a design has external validity, then the evaluator can also demonstrate that the program's results are applicable to participants in other places and at other times.

Internal validity is essential because, without it, the evaluator cannot tell if a finding is due to the program or some other factors or biases. For example, in an evaluation of a 5-year preventive health education program for high school students, the students may mature intellectually and emotionally, and this new maturity may be as important as the program in producing changes. This phenomenon is called "maturation." In addition to maturation, other common risks to internal validity include the following:

History. Historical events may occur that can bias the evaluation's results. For example, suppose a national campaign has been created to encourage people to make use of preventive health care services. If a change in health insurance laws favoring reimbursement for preventive health care occurs at the same time as the campaign, the evaluator will have difficulty separating the effects of the campaign from the effects resulting from increased access to care created by more favorable reimbursement for health care providers.

Instrumentation. Unless the measures used to collect data are dependable, the evaluator cannot be sure that the findings are accurate. For example, in a before-and-after design, an easier postmeasure than premeasure will erroneously favor the program. Untrained but lenient observers or test administrators can rule in favor of the program, while untrained but harsh observers or test administrators can rule against it.

Attrition. Sometimes the participants who remain in the evaluation are different from those who drop out.

Risks to an evaluation design's external validity are most often the consequence of the way in which participants are selected and assigned. For example, participants in an experimental evaluation can behave in atypical ways because they know they are in a special program; this is called the "Hawthorne effect." External validity is also risked when participants are tested, surveyed, or observed because they may become alerted to the kinds of behaviors that are expected or favored.

The Evaluation Design Report: Questions, Standards, and Independent Variables

The Evaluation Design Report (EDR) can be used in planning and explaining an evaluation. Designs begin with evaluation questions, standards, and independent variables, and the EDR depicts the relationship among them and the design.

The EDR shown in Figure 3.6 reports on the design for an 18-month program combining diet and exercise to improve health status and quality of life for persons 75 years of age or older. An experimental group of elderly people who still live at home will receive the program, while another group will not. Participants will be randomly assigned to the experimental or control groups according to the street on which they live. That is, participants living on Street A will be randomly assigned, as will participants living on Streets

B, C, and so on. Participants in the evaluation who need medical services can choose one of two clinics offering differing models of care, one that is primarily staffed by physicians and the other that is primarily staffed by nurses. The evaluators will be investigating whether any differences after

Evaluation Questions	Standards	Independent Variables	Evaluation Design
To what extent has quality of life improved?	A statistically and practically significant improvement in quality over a 1-year period A statistically and practically significant improvement in quality of life between male and female participants and nonparticipants with differing sociodemographic characteristics and health and functional status	Group participation, gender, patient mix	An experimental design with randomly assigned concurrent controls in which participating men and women of differing sociodemographic characteristics and health and functional status are compared over two periods of time
To what extent has health status improved?	A statistically and practically significant improvement in health over a 1-year period A statistically and practically significant improvement in quality of life between participants and nonparticipants with differing sociodemographic characteristics and health and functional status	Group, gender, patient mix	An experimental design with randomly assigned concurrent controls in which participating men and women of differing sociodemographic characteristics and health and functional status are compared over two periods of time

Figure 3.6. Evaluation Design Report

program participation exist for men and women and the role of patient mix in those differences.

The EDR shows that there are two evaluation questions. Each of the questions has two standards associated with it. The evaluation questions ask if the program has improved quality of life and health status and their independent variables are the same: group, gender, and patient mix. The evaluation will use an experimental design with randomly assigned concurrent controls. A pictorial representation of this design is shown in Figure 3.7.

Patient Mix	Gender	Time 1		Time 2	
		Experi-mental Participants	Control Participants	Experimental Participants	Control Participants
Very Complex Patient Mix	Men				
	Women				
Average Patient Mix	Men				
	Women				
Not Very Complex Patient Mix	Men				
	Women				

Figure 3.7. Experimental Evaluation Design and Randomly Assigned Concurrent Controls

SUMMARY AND TRANSITION TO THE NEXT CHAPTER ON SAMPLING

This chapter focused on ways to structure an evaluation so that program effects can be observed objectively. The structure includes the independent variables (such as the number and characteristics of the experimental and control groups) and number and timing of measures. The benefits and concerns associated with experimental and observational designs were discussed. A randomized trial is advocated if the evaluator wants to establish causation, but this design is difficult to implement. Although not as rigorous, nonrandomized trials and observational designs are useful and used by evaluators. The next chapter discusses sampling: What to do when you cannot obtain the entire population for the evaluation. Among the issues that will be discussed are how to obtain a random sample and how to select a large enough sample so that, if program differences exist, the evaluator will find them.

EXERCISE: EVALUATION DESIGN

Directions

Read the example below and identify the evaluation questions, standards, independent variables, and design. Comment on the potential for bias or error in your choice of evaluation design.

The Center for Refugee Health wants to find out if its 3-year program will result in improved quality of care. Among its strategies is to evaluate the appropriateness of pain management for children and other special populations (e.g., the elderly) before and after the program. A sample of patients and health care providers will be surveyed to find out their perceptions of the quality of care given and received.

Suggested Readings

Brett, A., & Grodin, M. (1991). Ethical aspects of human experimentation in health services research. *Journal of the American Medical Association, 265,* 1854-1857.

> This article is an extremely important one because it directs the evaluator's attention to the fact that the "participants" in experimental programs are human and that the requirements of informed consent apply as well as do concepts such as respect for privacy.

Campbell, D. T., & Stanley, J. C. (1963). *Experimental and quasi-experimental designs for research.* Chicago: Rand McNally.

> This is the classic book on differing research designs. "Threats" to internal and external validity are described in detail. Issues pertaining to generalizability and how to get at "truth" are important reading.

Dawson-Saunders, B., & Trapp, R. G. (1990). *Basic and clinical biostatistics.* East Norwalk, CT: Appleton & Lange.

> Chapter 2 discusses study designs in medical research and their advantages and disadvantages. Examples are given of the use of the designs.

Kosecoff, J., & Fink, A. (1982). *Evaluation basics.* Beverly Hills, CA: Sage

> Discusses alternative evaluation designs and threats to internal and external validity.

Review Notes

Purpose of This Chapter

This chapter discusses the reasons for sampling and explains the advantages and limitations of commonly used methods. These include random, systematic, stratified, cluster, and convenience sampling. The chapter also discusses the issues to consider in deciding on an appropriate sample size. A form for reporting on the sampling strategy is also examined. The report is designed to show the logical relationships among the evaluation questions, standards, independent variables, sampling strata, inclusion and exclusion criteria, dependent variables, measures, sampling methods, and size of the sample.

4 Sampling

What Is a Sample?

A **sample** is a portion or subset of a larger group called a **population**. The target population consists of the institutions, persons, problems, and systems to which or to whom the evaluation's findings are to be applied or "generalized." Consider the three target populations and samples in Example 4.1:

Example 4.1: Three Target Populations and Three Samples

1.
Target population: All homeless veterans throughout the United States

Program: Outreach, provision of single-room occupancy housing, medical and financial assistance, and job training: The REACH-OUT Program

Sample: 500 homeless veterans in four states who receive outpatient medical care between April 1 and June 30

Comment: The REACH-OUT Program is designed for all homeless veterans. The evaluator plans to select a sample of 500 homeless veterans in four states between April 1 and June 30. The findings are to be applied to all homeless veterans in all 50 states.

2.
Target population: All academic medical centers

Program: Continuous Quality Improvement: A program to monitor and change the system of care including its efficiency, one index of which is scheduling practices

Sample: A 10% sample, gathered over a 1-year period, of the records of all scheduled office visit times for patients with diabetes, hypertension, and depression in each of 20 medical centers

Comment: The target for this evaluation is all academic medical centers. Twenty medical centers will be selected for a Continuous Quality Improvement program. To appraise the program's efficiency, the evaluator will sample 10% of the records for patients with three medical conditions. The findings are to be applied to all medical centers.

3.
Target population: All newly diagnosed breast cancer patients

Program: Education in Options for Treatment

Sample: Five hospitals in three states; within each hospital, 15 physicians; for each physician, 20 patients seen between January 1 and July 31 who are newly diagnosed with breast cancer

Comment: Newly diagnosed women with breast cancer are the targets of an educational program. Between the months of January and July, the evaluators will select five hospitals and, within them, 20 patients for each of 15 doctors. The findings are to be applied to all patients with newly diagnosed breast cancer.

Inclusion and Exclusion Criteria or Eligibility

A sample is a constituent of a larger population to which the evaluation's findings will be applied. If an evaluation is intended to investigate the impact of an educational program on women's knowledge of their options for surgical treatment for cancer, for example, and not all women with cancer are to be included in the program, then the evaluator has to decide on the types of women who will be the focus of the study. Will the evaluation concentrate on women of a specific age? Women with a particular cancer? Example 4.2 contains hypothetical inclusion and exclusion criteria for an evaluation of such a program.

Example 4.2: Inclusion and Exclusion Criteria for a Sample of Women to Be Included in an Evaluation of a Program for Surgical Cancer Patients

Inclusion: Using the Medicare claims data base, of all patients hospitalized during 1993, those with diagnosis or procedure codes related to breast cancer; for patients with multiple admissions, only the admission with the most invasive operation

Exclusion: Women under the age of 65 (because women under 65 who receive Medicare are generally disabled or have renal disease), men, women with only a diagnostic biopsy or no breast surgery, women undergoing bilateral mastectomy, women without a code for primary breast cancer at the time of the most invasive operation, women with a diagnosis of carcinoma in situ, and women with metastases to regions other than the axillary lymph nodes

The evaluator of this program has set criteria for the sample of women who will be included in the evaluation and for which its conclusions will be appropriate. The sample will include women over 65 years of age who have been operated on for breast cancer. The findings of the evaluation will not be applicable to women under 65 with other types of cancer who have had only a diagnostic biopsy, have not had surgery, or have had bilateral mastectomy.

The independent variables are the evaluator's guide to determining where to set inclusion and exclusion criteria. For example, suppose that, in an evaluation of the effects on teens of a preventive health care program, one of the questions asks if boys and girls benefit equally from participation. In this evaluation question, the independent variable is gender and the dependent variable is benefit. If the evaluator plans to sample boys and girls, inclusion and exclusion criteria must be set. Hypothetical inclusion criteria could include boys and girls under 18 who are likely to attend all of the educational activities for the duration of the evaluation and who have a reading level appropriate for their age or grade. Teens might be excluded if they already participate in another preventive health care program, if they do not speak English, and if their parents object to their participation. If these hypothetical inclusion and exclusion criteria are used to guide sampling eligibility, then the evaluation's findings can be generalized only to English-speaking boys and girls under 18 who read at grade level and tend to be compliant with school attendance requirements. The findings are not designed to be applicable to teens who have difficulty reading or speaking English and who are unlikely to be able to complete all program activities.

Methods of Sampling

Sampling methods are usually divided into two types. The first is called **probability sampling,** and it is considered the best way to ensure the validity of any inferences made about a program's effectiveness and its generalizability. In probability sampling, every member of the target population has a known probability of being included in the sample.

The second type of sample is the **convenience sample** in which participants are selected because they are available. In convenience sampling, some members of the target population have a chance of being chosen, while others do not. As a result, the data that are collected from a convenience sample may not be applicable to the target group at all. For example, suppose an evaluator of the student health service decided to interview all students who came for care during the week of December 26. Suppose also that 100 students came and all agreed to be interviewed: a perfect response rate. The problem is that the end of December in some parts of the world is associated with respiratory viruses and skiing accidents; moreover, many universities are closed during that week and students are not around. Thus the data collected by the happy evaluator with the perfect response rate could very well be biased because the evaluation excluded many students simply because they were not on campus (and, if they were ill, received care elsewhere).

SIMPLE RANDOM SAMPLING

In simple random sampling, every subject or unit has an equal chance of being selected. Because of this equality of opportunity, random samples are considered relatively unbiased. Typical ways of selecting a simple random sample include using a table of random numbers or a computer-generated list of random numbers and applying them to lists of prospective participants.

Suppose an evaluator wanted to use a table and had the names of 20 physicians from which 10 were to be selected at random. First, the evaluator would assign a number to each name, 1 to 20 (e.g., Adams = 1; Baker = 2; . . . Thomas = 20). This list of numbers is called the **sampling frame.** Then, using a table of random numbers, which can be found in practically all statistics books, the evaluator would choose the first 10 digits between 1 and 20. Or a list of 10 numbers between 1 and 20 can be generated by the computer. Figure 4.1 illustrates the use of a table of random numbers in selecting a sample of 10 doctors from a list of 20.

One way to get a random sample: Using a table of random numbers. The evaluation team needed a randomly drawn sample of 10 physicians from a list of 20. Using a table of random numbers, they first identified a row of numbers at random and then a column. Where the two intersected, they began to identify their sample.

1 8 2 8 3	1 9 7 0 4²	4 5 3 8 7	2 3 4 7 6	1 2 3 2 3	3 4 8 6 5
4 6 4 5 3	2 1 5 4 7	3 9 2 4 6	9 3 1 9 8	9 8 0 0 5	6 5 9 8 8
1 9 0 7 6	2 3 4 5 3	3 2 7 6 0	2 7 1 6 6	7 5 0 3 2	9 9 9 4 5
3 6 7 4 3	8 9 5 6 3	*1 2* 3 7 8	9 8 2 2 3	2 3 4 6 5	2 5 4 0 8
2 2 1 2 5	1 9 7 8 6	2 3 4 9 8	7 6 5 7 5	7 6 4 3 5	6 3 4 4 2
7 6 0 0 9	7 7 0 9 9	4 3 7 8 8	3 6 6 5 9	7 4 3 9 9	*0 3* 4 3 2
0 9 8 7 8	7 6 5 4 9	8 8 8 7 7	2 6 5 8 7	4 4 6 3 3	7 7 6 5 9
3 4 5 3 4	4 4 4 7 5	5 6 6 3 2	3 4 3 5 0	*0 1* 7 6 8	2 9 0 2 7
8 3 1 0 9	7 5 8 9 9	3 4 8 7 7	2 1 3 5 7	2 4 3 0 0	0 0 8 6 9
8 9 0 6 3	4 3 5 5 5	3 2 7 0 0	7 6 4 9 7	3 6 0 9 9	9 7 9 5 6
				9 4 6 5 6	3 4 6 8 9
0 9 8 8 7	6 7 7 7 0	6 9 9 7 5	5 4 4 6 5	*1 3* 8 9 6	*0 4* 6 4 5
2 3 2 8 0	3 4 5 7 2	9 9 4 4 3	9 8 7 6 5	3 4 9 7 8	4 2 8 8 0
9 3 8 5 6	2 3 0 9 0	2 2 2 5 7	6 7 4 0 0	2 3 5 8 0	2 4 3 7 6
2 1 2 5 6	5 0 8 6 3	5 6 9 3 4	7 0 9 9 3	3 4 7 6 5	3 0 9 9 6
1 4 5 7 5¹	3 5 4 9 0³	2 3 6 4 5	2 2 1 7 9	3 5 7 8 8	3 7 6 0 0
2 3 2 7 6	7⁴0 8 7 0	*2 0* 0 8 7	6 6 6 6 5	7 8 8 7 6	5 8 0 0 7
8 7 5 3 0	4 5 7 3 8	*0 9* 9 9 8	4 5 3 9 7	4 7 5 0 0	3 4 8 7 5
0 0 7 9 1	3 2 1 6 4	9 7 6 6 5	2 7 5 8 9	9 0 0 8 7	*1 6* 0 0 4
9 9 0 0 3	3 2 5 6 7	*0 2* 8 7 8	3 8 6 0 2	*1 8* 7 0 0	2 3 4 5 5
1 4 3 6 7	6 4 9 9 9	7 8 4 5 3	4 0 0 7 8	5 3 7 2 7	2 8 7 5 9

1 = Two rolls of a die yield 1 (column) and 5 (block)
2 = Two rolls of a die yield 2 (column) and 1 (row)
3 = Intersection of ¹ and ²
4 = Start here to get the sample

Figure 4.1. A Portion of a Table of Random Numbers

NOTE: Numbers that are **bold** and underlined = sample of ten, consisting of numbers between 1 and 20.

1. How they randomly identified the row. A member of the evaluation team tossed a die twice. The first die was 3, and the second was 5. Starting with the first column, this corresponded to the third block and the fifth row of that block, or number 1 4 5 7 5.

2. How they randomly identified the column. A member of the team tossed the die twice and got a 2 and 1. This identified the second block of columns and the first column beginning with 1. The starting point for this sample is where the row 1 4 5 7 5 and the column beginning with 1 intersect, at 3 5 4 9 0.

3. How the sample was chosen. The evaluation team needed 10 physicians from their list of 20—or two-digit numbers. Moving down from column 2, the ten numbers between 1 and 20 that appear (starting with the numbers below 3 5 4 9 0, and beginning with the first number, 7) are 12, 20, 09, 01, 13, 18, 03, 04, and 16. These are the physicians that constitute the random sample.

RANDOM SELECTION AND RANDOM ASSIGNMENT

In any given evaluation, random selection may be a different process than random assignment, as is illustrated in Example 4.3:

Example 4.3: Random Selection and Random Assignment: Two Examples

1. Evaluation A had 6 months to identify a sample of teens to participate in an evaluation of an innovative school-based preventive health care program. At the end of the 6 months, all eligible teens were assigned to the innovative or the traditional (control) program. Assignment was based on how close to a participating school each teen lived. This method was used because participation meant that students are required to attend several after-school activi-

ties, and no funding was available for transportation.

2. Evaluator B had 6 months to identify a sample of teens to participate in an evaluation of an innovative school-based preventive health care program. At the end of the 6 months, a sample was randomly selected from all who were eligible. Half the sample was randomly assigned to the innovative and half to the traditional (control) program.

In the first situation, the evaluator selected all eligible teens and then assigned them to the experimental and control groups according to how close they lived to a participating school. In the second example, the evaluator selected a random sample of all those who were eligible and then randomly assigned them to an experimental or control group. The second situation is usually considered preferable to the first. Random selection means that every eligible person has an equal chance; if all are included because they just happened to appear during the time allocated for sampling, biases may be introduced. Random assignment can also guard against bias.

SYSTEMATIC SAMPLING

Suppose an evaluator had a list with the names of 3,000 nurse practitioners, from which a sample of 500 was to be selected. In **systematic sampling,** 3,000 would be divided by 500 to yield 6, and every sixth name would be selected. An alternative would be to select a number at random, say, by tossing dice. Suppose a toss came up with the number 5. Then the fifth name would be selected first, then the tenth, fifteenth, and so on until 500 names were selected.

Systematic sampling should not be used if repetition is a natural component of the sampling frame. For example, if the frame is a list of names, those beginning with certain letters of the alphabet might get excluded because, for certain ethnicities, they appear infrequently.

STRATIFIED SAMPLING

A **stratified random sample** is one in which the population is divided into subgroups or "strata," and a random sample is then selected from each group. For example, in a program to teach women about options for treatment for breast cancer, the evaluator might choose to sample women of differing general health status (as indicated by scores on a 32-item test), age, and income (high = +; medium = 0, and low = −). Health status, age, and income are the strata. This sampling blueprint can be depicted as follows (Figure 4.2):

Health Status Scores and Income	Age (years)				
	< 35	35-55	56-65	66-75	>75
25-32 Points					
High income					
Average					
Low					
17-24 Points					
High income					
Average					
Low					
9-16 Points					
High income					
Average					
Low					
1-8 Points					
High income					
Average					
Low					

Figure 4.2. Sampling Blueprint for a Program to Educate Women in Options for Breast Cancer Treatment

The strata or subgroups are chosen because the evaluator has reason to believe that they are related to the dependent variable or outcome measure; in this case, the options chosen by women with breast cancer. That is, the evaluator has evidence that general health status, age, and income influence a women's choice of treatment.

The justification for the selection of the strata must be evidence from the literature or other sources of information (such as historical data or expert opinion). If the evaluator neglects to use stratification in the choice of a sample, the final results may be confounded. For example, if the evaluation neglects to distinguish among women with different characteristics, good and poor performance may be averaged among them, and the program will seem to have no effect even if one or more groups benefited. In fact, the program actually might have been very successful with certain women, say, those over 75, with General Health Status scores between 25 and 32 and with a moderate income.

When stratification is not used, statistical techniques (such as analysis of covariance and regression) may be applied retrospectively (after the data have already been collected) to correct for confounders or "covariates" on the dependent variables or outcomes. Evaluators generally agree, however, that it is better to anticipate confounding variables by sampling prospectively than to correct for them by analysis, retrospectively. The reason is that statistical corrections require very strict assumptions about the nature of the data, assumptions for which the sampling plan may not have been designed. With few exceptions, using statistical corrections afterward results in a loss of power or ability to detect true differences between groups like the experimental and control groups.

The **strata** are subsets of the independent variables. If the independent variables are gender, health status, and education, the strata are how you define each one. For example, gender is defined as male and female. A variable such as health status can be defined in may ways, depending on the measures available to collect data and the needs of the evaluation. For example, health status may be defined as a score on some measure or judged to be excellent, very good, good, fair, or poor.

CLUSTER SAMPLING

Cluster sampling is used in large evaluations: those that involve many settings, such as universities, hospitals, cities, states, and so on. In **cluster sampling,** the population is divided into batches. The batches can be randomly selected and assigned, and their constituents can be randomly selected and assigned. For example, suppose that California's counties are trying out a new program to improve emergency care for critically ill and injured children; the control program is the traditional emergency medical system. If you want to use random cluster sampling, you can consider each county to be a cluster and select and assign counties at random to the new or traditional programs. Alternatively, you can randomly select children's hospitals and other facilities treating critically ill children within counties and randomly assign them to the experimental or the traditional system (assuming this were considered ethical).

Example 4.4 gives an illustration of the use of cluster sampling in a survey of Italian parents' attitudes toward AIDS.

Example 4.4: Cluster Sampling and Attitudes of Italian Parents to AIDS

Epidemiologists from 14 of Italy's 21 regions surveyed parents of 725 students from 30 schools chosen by a cluster sample technique of the 292 classical, scientific, and technical high schools in Rome. Staff visited the schools and selected students using a list of random numbers based on the school's size. Each of the selected students was given a letter addressed to the parents explaining the goals of the study and when they would be contacted.

NONPROBABILITY OR CONVENIENCE SAMPLES

Convenience samples are those for which the probability of selection is unknown. Evaluators use convenience samples simply because they are easy to get. This means that some people have no chance at all of being selected, simply because they are not around to be chosen. These samples are considered biased, or not representative of the target population, unless proven otherwise.

In some cases, statistical analyses can be performed to demonstrate that a convenience sample is really representative. For example, suppose during the months of July and August, an evaluator conducts a survey of the needs of county institutions concerned with critically ill and injured children. Because those are months during which some county employees take vacations, the respondents may be different than those who would answer the survey during the rest of the year. For example, the July-and-August people who respond may have been on the job for less time, not eligible for vacation, and, perhaps, less experienced too. If the evaluator wants to demonstrate that the two samples (those who were around to respond and those who were not) are not different, the two groups can be compared on key variables such as time on the job and experience with critically ill and injured children. If no differences are found, then the evaluator is in a relatively stronger position to assert that, even though the sample was chosen on the basis of convenience, its characteristics do not differ on certain key variables (such as length of time on the job) from the target population's.

The Sampling Unit

A major concern in sampling is the "unit" to be sampled. Consider Example 4.5:

Example 4.5: What Is the Target? Who Is Sampled?

An evaluation of a new program is concerned with identifying its effectiveness in altering physicians' practices pertaining to acute pain management for children who have undergone an operation. The target population is all physicians who care for children undergoing an operation. The evaluation question is this: "Have physicians improved their pain management practices for children?" The standards are that physicians in the experimental group show significant improvement over a 1-year period and significantly greater improvement than a control. Resources are available for 20 physicians to participate in the evaluation.

Ten physicians will be randomly assigned to the experimental group and ten will be assigned to the control. The evaluator plans to find out about pain management through a review of the medical records of ten patients of each of the physicians in the experimental and control groups for a total sample of 200 patients. (This is sometimes called a "nested design.") A consultant to the evaluation team says that, in actuality, the evaluation is really comparing the practices of 10 physicians against those of 10 physicians, and not the care of 100 patients against that of 100 patients. The reason is that characteristics of the care of the patients of any single physician will be very highly related. The consultant advises correcting for this lack of "independence among patients of the same physician" by using one of the statistical methods available for correcting for "cluster" effects. A contradictory consultant advises using a much larger number of patients per physician and suggests a statistical method for selecting the appropriate number. Because the evaluator does not have enough money to enlarge the sample, a decision is made to "correct" statistically for the dependence among patients.

In the example above, the evaluator wants to apply the evaluation's findings to all physicians but only has resources to include 20 in the evaluation. In an ideal world, the evaluator would have access to a very large number of physicians. In this less-than-ideal world, however, the evaluator has resources to study 10 patients per physician and access to statistical methods to correct for possible biases. These statistical methods enable evaluators to provide remedies for the possible dependence among the patients of a single physician, among students at a single institution, among health care workers at a single hospital, and so on.

The Size of the Sample

POWER ANALYSIS AND ALPHA AND BETA ERRORS

An evaluation's ability to detect an effect is its power. A **power analysis** is a statistical method of identifying a sample size that is large enough to detect the effect, if one actually exists.

A commonly used evaluation research design is one in which two randomly assigned groups are compared to find out if differences exist between them. "Does Program A differ from Program B in its ability to improve quality of life?" is, accordingly, a typical evaluation question. To answer the question accurately, the evaluator must be sure that enough people are in each program group so that, if a difference is actually present, it will be uncovered. Conversely, if there is no difference between the two groups, the evaluator does not want to conclude falsely that there is one. To begin the process of making sure that the evaluation's sample size is adequate to detect any true differences, the first step is to reframe the appropriate evaluation questions into null hypotheses. Null hypotheses state that no difference exists between groups, as illustrated in Example 4.6:

Example 4.6: The Null Hypothesis in a Program to Improve Quality of Life

Question: Does Experimental Program A improve quality of life?

Standard: A statistically significant difference is found in quality of life between Experimental Program A's participants and Control Program B's. The difference is in Program A's favor.

Data source: The Quality of Life Assessment, a 30-minute self-administered questionnaire, with 100 questions—scoring ranges from 1 to 100 with 100 meaning excellent quality of life

Null hypothesis: No difference in quality of life exists for participants in Program A and in Program B (that is, the average scores obtained in Program A and in Program B are equal).

One accepted way of identifying a sample that is large enough to detect actual effects is to use a method called **power analysis.** The power of an experimental evaluation is its ability to detect a true difference; in other words, to detect a difference of a given size (say, 10%) if the difference actually exists.

When an evaluator finds differences existing among programs, and, in reality, there are no differences, that is called an **alpha** or **Type I error.** Type I errors are analogous to a false-positive test that indicates, incorrectly, that a disease is present when it is not. When an evaluator finds no differences among programs, although in reality there are differences, that is termed a **beta** or **Type II error.** Type II errors are analogous to a false-negative test that indicates, incorrectly, that a disease is not present when it is. The relationship between what the evaluator finds and the true situation can be depicted as follows (Figure 4.3):

Truth

		Differences exist	No differences exist
Evaluator's conclusions from hypothesis test	Differences exist (Reject null)	Correct	Type I or alpha error
	No differences exist (Keep null)	Type II or beta error	Correct

Figure 4.3. Type I and Type II Errors: Searching for a True Difference

Selection of a sample size that will maximize an evaluation's power relies on formulas whose use requires understanding hypothesis testing and having a basic knowledge of statistics. The formulas usually require

- stating the null hypothesis;
- setting a level (alpha or α) of statistical significance—usually .05 or .01—and deciding whether it is to be a one- or two-tailed test;
- deciding on the smallest meaningful health-related difference (e.g., the difference in average scores between groups must be at least 15 points);
- setting the power $(1 - \beta)$ of the evaluation or the chance of detecting a difference (usually 80% or 90%); and
- estimating the standard deviation (assuming that the distribution of the measure is normal) in the population.

Alternative sample size calculations have been proposed based on confidence intervals. A confidence interval is computed from sample data that have a given probability that the unknown parameter (such as the mean) is contained within the interval. Common confidence intervals are 90%, 95%, and 99%.

Why Sample?

Evaluators sample because to do so is efficient and precise. Samples can be studied more quickly than target populations, and they are also less expensive to assemble. In some cases, recruiting a complete population for an evaluation is probably impossible, even if time and financial resources are available. For example, enrolling all homeless veterans in an investigation of a program targeted to them is futile (see Example 4.1, page 70).

Sampling also is efficient in that resources that might go into collecting data on an unnecessarily large number of individuals or groups can be spent on other evaluation activities such as monitoring the quality of data collection and standardizing the implementation of the program.

Sampling enables the evaluator to focus on precisely the characteristics of interest. For example, suppose an evaluator wants to compare older and younger patients with differing health and functional status. A stratified sampling strategy can give the evaluator just what is needed. A sample of the population with precise characteristics is more suitable for many evaluations than the entire population.

The Sampling Report

The Sampling Report (SR) can be used in planning and explaining an evaluation. The report contains the evaluation questions and standards, the independent variables and strata, the evaluation design, inclusion and exclusion criteria, the dependent variable, the measure, the criteria for level of acceptable statistical and clinical (or educational or practical) significance, the sampling methods, and the size of the sample.

Figure 4.4 illustrates the use of the SR for one evaluation question asked in an 18-month program combining diet and exercise to improve health status and quality of life for persons 75 years of age or older. An experimental group of elderly people who still live at home will receive the program, while another group will not. To be eligible, participants must be able to live independently and feed, clothe, and shop for themselves. Persons who are under 65 years of age and do not speak English or Spanish are not eligible. Participants will be randomly assigned to the experimental or control groups according to the street on which they live. That is, participants living on Street A will be randomly assigned as will participants living on Streets B, C, and so on. The evaluators will be investigating whether the program effectively improves quality of life for men and women equally. A random sample of men and women will be selected from all who are eligible, but no two will live on the same street. Then men and women will be assigned at random to the experimental or control group.

The Evaluation	The Report
Evaluation Questions	1. To what extent has quality of life improved? 2. Do men and women differ in quality of life after participation?
Standard	1. A statistical and clinically meaningful difference between experimental and control group, favoring the experimental group 2. Thus no standard is necessary. If differences between men and women are found, they will be examined to determine if they are clinically meaningful.
Evaluation Design	An experimental design, with randomly assigned concurrent controls
Independent Variables	Group participation; gender
Strata	Group participation: experimental and control Gender: male and female
Inclusion Criteria	1. Must be living at home 2. Must be functionally independent (e.g., can feed, clothe, and shop for themselves)
Exclusion criteria	1. Unable to speak English or Spanish 2. Under 65 years of age
Dependent Variable	Quality of life
Measure	Quality of Life Questionnaire: a 100-point survey. The questionnaire's manual states that, when used with persons over 70 years, the standard deviation (a measure of how much the score "spread" from the mean or average score) is 10 points.
Criterion for Clinical Meaning	A difference of at least 5 points on the Quality of Life Questionnaire between experimental and control, favoring the experimental group. Statistical significance (alpha) = .01; power is 80% (beta = .20).

Figure 4.4. Sampling Report Form

The Evaluation	The Report
Sampling Method	For group assignment: Cluster sampling. All streets in the town are eligible. All eligible persons in a given street are randomly assigned to the experimental or control group. For gender: An equal number of men and women will be randomly selected from all who are eligible; men and women will be randomly assigned to an experimental or a control group. No two participants will live on the same street.
Sample Size	To compare men and women, a total of 188 people are needed: 94 men and 94 women; 47 of each will be assigned to the experimental or control groups.

Figure 4.4. (Continued)

SUMMARY AND TRANSITION TO THE NEXT CHAPTER ON DATA COLLECTION

The next chapter discusses the issues involved in collecting evaluation data and describes and analyzes the sources of information available for evaluators. In the previous two chapters on evaluation research design and sampling, the evaluator focused on the independent or predictor variables. These often consist of groups (e.g., experimental and control), demographic characteristics, and settings (e.g., teaching and community-based hospitals).

Associated with research design are the issues of sampling. Is sampling appropriate? Who should be sampled? How many people should be in each group? How will they be selected and assigned? Once these questions are answered, the evaluator shifts emphasis to data collection, the topic of the next two chapters.

In the next chapter, the sources of information available to the evaluator are discussed, as are their advantages and limitations. In evaluations, data are collected to describe participants as well as to measure the effects of the program on health, education, and quality and efficiency of care.

EXERCISE: SAMPLING

Directions

1. Choose the sampling method used in each of the following situations.
   Choices:
   A. Simple random sampling
   B. Stratified sampling
   C. Cluster sampling
   D. Systematic sampling
   E. Convenience sampling

Situation	Choice (Write in Letter)
1. The Rehabilitation Center has 40 separate family counseling groups, each with about 30 participants. The director of the Center has noticed a decline in attendance rates and has decided to try out an experimental program to improve them. The program is very expensive, and the center's directors can afford to finance only a 250-person program at first. Randomly selecting individuals from all group members will create friction and disturb the integrity of some of the groups. As an alternative, the evaluator has suggested a plan in which five of the groups--150 people--will be randomly selected to take part in the experimental program and five will participate in the control.	-- -- -- -- -- --
2. The Medical Center has developed a new program to teach patients about cardiovascular fitness. The evaluation is determining how effective the program is with males and females of different ages. The evaluation design is experimental, with concurrent controls. In it, the new and traditional cardiovascular programs are compared. About 310 people signed up for the winter seminar. Of the 310, 140 are between 45 and 60 years old and 62 of these were men. The remaining 170 are between 61 and 75 years old, and 80 of these are men. The evaluators randomly selected 40 persons from each of the four subgroups and randomly assigned every other person to the new program and the remainder to the old program.	-- -- -- -- -- --
3. Two hundred health education teachers signed up for a continuing education program. Only 50, however, are to participate in an evaluation of the program's impact. Each participant is assigned a number from 001 to 200 and, using a table, 50 names are selected by moving down columns of three-digit random numbers and taking the first 50 numbers within the range 001 to 200.	-- -- -- -- -- --

Suggested Readings

Bailar, J. C., & Mosteller, F. (1988). Guidelines for statistical reporting in articles for medical journals. *Annals of Internal Medicine, 108,* 266-273.

> The authors explain the logic behind discussing the eligibility of experimental participants and the relationship between who is included and the population about whom inferences are to be made. The authors also describe the characteristics of comprehensible reporting about randomization, blinding, and losses to observation.

Centers for Disease Control. (1992). *Journal of the American Medical Association, 267,* 2160.

> Describes the cluster sampling method used in a survey of Italian parents' attitudes toward AIDS.

Dawson-Saunders, B., & Trapp, R. G. (1990). *Basic and clinical biostatistics.* East Norwalk, CT: Appleton & Lange.

> A basic and essential primer on the use of statistics in medicine and medical care settings. Explains study designs and sampling. In addition to very clear explanations of the statistics involved in sampling, the authors provide numerous examples.

Lachin, J. M. (1981). Introduction to sample size determination and power analysis for clinical trials. *Controlled Clinical Trials, 2,* 93-113.

> Explains the logic behind sample size determination.

Purpose of This Chapter

This chapter covers the criteria for choosing among differing sources of evaluation information (including self-administered questionnaires, achievement tests, medical record reviews, observations, interviews, large data bases (such as Medicare data tapes, vital statistics), performance tests, clinical scenarios, physical examinations and the literature and discusses their advantages and limitations. Special emphasis is given to reviewing the published literature for information because of the importance of reviews to competent evaluations. The next chapter covers how to evaluate the reliability and validity of existing measures of important health variables; the construction, selection, and coding of items and scales; and the preparation of a data collection plan.

5 Collecting Information: The Right Data Sources

A Reader's Guide to Chapter 5

Information Sources: What's the Problem?

Choosing the Best Sources

Sources of Data and Their Advantages and Limitations:
Self-administered surveys, tests of achievement, medical
record reviews, observations, interviews, physical
examinations, vital statistics and uniform data bases,
performance tests, clinical scenarios, and the literature

Information Sources: What's the Problem?

An evaluator is asked to study the effectiveness of an intervention whose main objectives include providing a high quality of health care and improving the health status and quality of life for elderly persons over 75 years of age who are still living at home—the At-Home Program. The experimental intervention consists of a comprehensive assessment of each older person by an interdisciplinary team of health care providers and a home visit every 3 months by a nurse practitioner to monitor progress and reevaluate health and function. The control group consists of elderly people in the same community who are not visited by the nurse practitioner and continue with their usual sources of care. What information should the evaluator collect to find out if the intervention's objectives have been achieved? Where should the information come from? The evaluation questions and standards and their associated independent and dependent variables are the first place to go for answers. Consider these examples from the evaluation of the At-Home Program:

Example 5.1: Evaluation Questions, Standards, Variables, and Data Sources

Evaluation question 1: Has quality of care improved for diabetic patients?

Standard: A statistically and clinically meaningful improvement in quality of care is observed in experimental as compared with control diabetic patients.

Independent variable: Group participation (experimental diabetics and control diabetics)

Potential data sources: Physical examination, medical record review, surveys of health care practitioners and patients

Dependent variable: Quality of care

Potential data sources: Medical record review, surveys of health care practitioners and patients

Evaluation question 2: Is quality of life improved?

Standard: One aspect of good quality of life is sociability. Evidence of sociability for the program is a statistically significant difference between the experimental and control group in their sociability, favoring the experimental group.

Independent variable: Group participation (experimental and control)

Potential data source: Names or ID codes of participants in the experimental and control groups

Dependent variable: Sociability

Potential data sources: Surveys of patients, families, and friends; surveys of health care practitioners; reviews of diaries kept by patients; observations

---

Answering the first question in Example 5.1 pertaining to quality of care and diabetic patients has at least two implicit tasks: identifying persons with diabetes and assigning them to the experimental and control groups. Patients with diabetes can be identified through physical examination, medical record review, or surveys of health care practitioners and patients. Quality of care for diabetes can be measured by reviewing medical records or surveying health care practitioners.

To identify persons in the experimental and control groups for the second question, a review of the sampling logs is sufficient. To measure sociability, the evaluator can survey and observe patients, ask them to keep records or diaries of their activities, and survey health care practitioners.

Given the range of choices for each evaluation question, on what basis does the evaluator choose to interview the family rather than administer a questionnaire to the study's participants? How does the evaluator decide between medical record reviews and physical exams? Answering these questions is at the heart of a program evaluation's data collection.

Choosing the Best Source of Data

Evaluators have access to an arsenal of information-collection sources. Among them are self-administered questionnaires, tests of performance and achievement, face-to-face and telephone interviews, observations, large data bases, vital statistics (such as infant mortality rates), the literature, and personal, medical, financial, and other statistical records. Each has its advantages and limitations. To choose a source of data, use these guidelines to ask the following questions:

Guidelines for Questions to Ask in Choosing a Data Source

- What variables need to be measured? Are they defined and specific enough to measure?
- Can you borrow or adapt a currently available measure, or must a new measure be created?
- If an available measure seems to be appropriate, has it been tried out in circumstances that are similar to the current evaluation's?
- Do you have the technical skills, financial resources, and time to create a valid measure?
- If no measure is available or appropriate, can you develop one in the time allocated for the evaluation?
- Do you have the technical skills, financial resources, and time to collect information with the chosen measure?
- Are participants likely to be able to fill out forms, answer questions, and provide information called for by the measure?
- In studies that involve direct services to patients and use of information from medical and other confidential records, can you obtain permission to collect data in an ethical way?
- To what extent will users of the evaluation's results (e.g., practitioners, students, patients, program developers, and sponsors) have confidence in the sources of information on which they are based?

Example 5.2 shows what can happen when evaluators neglect to answer these questions.

Example 5.2: (Not) Collecting Evaluation Information: A Case Study

The evaluators of an innovative third-year core surgery clerkship prepared a written examination to find out if students learned to test donor-recipient compatibility before transfusion of red blood cells. The examination (to be given before and after the clerkship) included questions about the mechanisms involved in and consequences of transfusing incompatible red cells, the causes of incompatible transfusions, what to do about RH negative females who may bear children, how to identify unusual red cell antibodies, and what to do when no compatible blood is available.

The evaluators also prepared a measure of students' understanding of ethical issues in blood transfusion. The measure consisted of 10 hypothetical scenarios with ethical components, and the idea was to compare students' responses to standards of ethics set by the University Blood Bank.

Finally, the evaluators anticipated distributing a self-administered survey to students to find out if their attitudes toward transfusion medicine changed before and after their participation in the clerkship. The results of the evaluators' activities were to be presented at a special meeting of the School of Medicine's Curriculum Committee one year after the start of the innovative program.

The evaluators' report turned out to be very brief. Although they were able to locate a number of achievement tests with questions about donor-recipient compatibility, and thus did not have to prepare them from "scratch," they could not find an appropriate time to give all students a premeasure and postmeasure. This meant that the evaluators had incomplete information on the performance of many students, with only pretests for some and only posttests for others. In addition, the evaluators found that developing the scenarios took about 9 months because they were more difficult to compile than had been anticipated.

A sample of students found the scenarios hard to understand and ambiguous. The evaluators had to rewrite and retest the scenarios, and they were not even ready for use at reporting time.

Finally, many students refused to complete the attitude questionnaire. Anecdotal information suggested that students felt they were overloaded with tests and questionnaires and that these additional ones did not seem to be important. Because of the poor quality of the data, the evaluators were unable to provide any meaningful information about the third-year surgery clerkship's progress.

In the case study presented above, the evaluators encountered difficulties for these reasons:

- Not enough time to collect data on students' achievement before and after
- Not enough time and possibly a lack of skills in preparing the scenarios
- Choice of information collection method that was not appropriate for the participants because they were unwilling to complete it

Sources of Data in Program Evaluation and Their Advantages and Limitations

The following is a description of the characteristics, advantages, and limitations of 10 of the most commonly used sources of data in evaluations.

1. SELF-ADMINISTERED SURVEYS

Self-administered surveys (also called questionnaires) ask individuals to answer questions or respond to items. The answers are typically recorded directly on the survey. A typical survey item might look like this:

	Yes	No
During the past 4 weeks, have you had any of the following problems with your work or other regular daily activities as a result of any emotional problems (such as feeling depressed or anxious)? Please answer YES or NO for each question by circling 1 or 2 on each line.		
Cut down the amount of time you spent on work or other activities?	1	2
Accomplished less than you would like?	1	2
Didn't do work or other activities as usual?	1	2

Figure 5.1. Self-Administered Survey Item

Advantages:

- Many people are accustomed to completing surveys.
- Many surveys and rating scales are available for adaptation.
- Self-administered surveys are conducive to confidentiality and anonymity.
- Surveys can be administered to large groups of people at relatively low cost.

Disadvantages:

- The people who respond (called the **respondents**) may not always tell the truth.
- The self-administered survey's format is not suitable for obtaining explanations of behavior or sensitive information.
- Without supervision, some respondents may fail to answer some or even all questions.

2. TESTS OF ACHIEVEMENT

The most commonly used method of collecting information on educational accomplishment is the written achievement test. Written tests tend to measure knowledge, understanding, and application of theories, principles, and facts. To assess higher levels of learning such as the evaluation of evidence or the synthesis of information from varying sources, other methods, such as observation of performance or analysis of written papers and scientific studies, are more appropriate.

Most evaluations of educational programs rely to some extent on written tests of achievement, and many of these are multiple choice:

Multiple-Choice Question on an Achievement Test

What is the best medical therapy for a patient experiencing a mild urticarial reaction from blood transfusion? **Please circle one choice only.**

Steroids.	1
Antihistamines.	2
Lasix.	3
Epinephrine.	4
Aspirin.	5

3. MEDICAL RECORD REVIEWS

Medical record reviews are used in audits of medical practices and in research that aims to study the quality of medical care. Figure 5.2 is a component of a medical record to find out about adverse outcomes for patients admitted to the hospital with a heart attack.

Advantages:

  ◆ Collecting data from medical records can be relatively unobtrusive in that office and hospital procedures need not be disturbed.
  ◆ If you need data on actual practice (e.g., performance of procedures, medications prescribed), this is an excellent source.
  ◆ If data are needed on some patient demographic characteristics (e.g., age, sex, insurance status, medical history), this may be an accurate source.

Disadvantages:

  ◆ Finding information in the record can make this a time-consuming activity.

VII. Physician Care

**Answers should be based on
physicians' notes including history and
physical, consult reports, progress notes,
and ER [emergency room] notes.**

Adverse Outcomes

Did a physician document the occurrence of the following adverse outcomes <u>during</u> the marker admission for hospitalized Medicare patients with myocardial infarction [heart attack]? If so, give the date when each was <u>first</u> noted.

Adverse Outcome	Occur During Admission?		If YES, Give Date (nd=9999)
	Yes	No/nd	Mo/Day
i. Chest pain on day 3 or later, and present for at least two consecutive days.	1	9	-- -- -- --
ii. Shock beginning on day 2, or later (physician notes patient developed shock or had a systolic BP < 90).	1	9	-- -- -- --
iii. Arrest (cardiac, respiratory or unspecified, sudden death, CPR or resuscitation); exclude arrests in ER.	1	9	-- -- -- --
iv. Death.	1	9	-- -- -- --
v. Insertion of temporary or permanent pacemaker.	1	9	-- -- -- --

Check here if none of the above adverse outcomes occurred: [-------]

Figure 5.2. Portion of a Medical Record Review Form: Adverse Outcomes for Medicare Patients Admitted to the Hospital with a Heart Attack

- ◆ You must be sure that the review process is reliable and accurate. This may mean training people to do the reviews or developing and validating review forms, and training is time-consuming and expensive.
- ◆ Certain types of information are not always in the record, (e.g., patients' functional or mental status).

♦ The record does not provide data on the appropriateness of practice or on the relationship between what was done by the practitioner (the process of care) and patient results (the outcomes of care).

4. OBSERVATIONS

Observations are appropriate for describing the environment (e.g., the size of an examination room or the number, types, and dates of magazines in the office waiting room) and for obtaining global portraits of the dynamics of a situation (e.g., a typical problem-solving session among medical students or a "day in the life" of a clinic). A commonly used observational technique is the time-and-motion study in which measures are taken of the amount of time spent by patients and physicians as they go through the health care system. Usually, time-and-motion studies are used to measure the efficiency of care. The following is a portion of a typical observation form:

	Circle One
Is the waiting room carpeted?	
Yes, all areas	1
Yes, some areas	2
No, no areas	3
Do the windows have drapes or blinds?	
Yes	1
No	2
Not applicable because no windows	3

Figure 5.3. Portion of an Observation Form

Advantages:

♦ Observations provide an opportunity to collect firsthand information.
♦ Observations can provide information of potential importance that cannot be anticipated.

Disadvantages:

♦ A very structured format and extensive training are required for dependable observations.
♦ Observations are labor-intensive and time-consuming.
♦ The observer can influence the environment being studied, and people can act different from usual because they are being "watched."

5. INTERVIEWS

Interviews can be conducted in person and on the telephone. The following is an excerpt from a typical patient face-to-face interview:

---

9. **ASK:** Have you ever been told by a doctor, nurse, or other health care professional that you had a heart attack, myocardial infarction (MI), or coronary?

[ ] No: **GO TO QUESTION 10**

[ ] Yes: **CONTINUE**

9a **ASK:** How long ago did you have your heart attack, myocardial infarction (MI) or coronary? (**Read list to patient. SAY:** Before you answer, I will read you a list.)

[ ] Less than one month

[ ] 1-2 months

[ ] 2-3 months

[ ] 3-6 months

[ ] 6-9 months

[ ] 9-12 months

[ ] More than 12 months

9b. **ASK:** Since your most recent heart attack was diagnosed, have you had any further episodes of angina (chest pain)? **SAY:** Before you answer, I will read you a list.

[ ] Yes, more than 1 a day

[ ] Yes, about 1 a day

[ ] Yes, about 1 a week

[ ] Yes, about 1 a month

[ ] No

Figure 5.4. Portion of an Interview Form

Advantages:

- Interviews allow individuals to ask about the meaning of questions.
- Interviews can collect information from people who may have difficulty reading or seeing.

Disadvantages:

- Interviews are time-consuming and labor-intensive.
- Interviewers require extensive training and monitoring.
- Special skills may be required to interpret responses that are "off the record."

6. PHYSICAL EXAMINATIONS

Physical examinations are invaluable sources of data for evaluators because they produce primary data on health status. Physical examinations for evaluation purposes may intrude on the time and privacy of the physician and the patient, however, and, because they are labor-intensive, they are an expensive data source.

Because of the possibility that an examination will be conducted or received differently if physicians and patients are aware that they are in an experiment, "blinding" is recommended for evaluations. With blinding, participants consent to be in an experimental study, but they do not know whether they are in the experimental or a comparison group. A double-blinded evaluation means that neither physicians nor patients know their group; a single-blinded evaluation means that one type of participant knows.

7. VITAL STATISTICS AND UNIFORM DATA BASES

The National Center for Health Statistics, the Agency for Health Care Policy and Research, the Centers for Disease Control and Prevention (CDC), and the U.S. Bureau of the Census are among the agencies that make data tapes and published statistical reports available to the public. The National Center for Health Statistics (NCHS), for example, has data systems that include a Vital Registration system (e.g., reporting systems that include deaths, fetal deaths, birth registrations, marriage registrations, divorce registration, and abortions). Data are published in *Vital Statistics of the United States.*

The NCHS also has surveys based on the registration systems, and these include the National Maternal and Infant Health Survey (with data collected by the U.S. Census Bureau) and the national Mortality Followback Surveys. Finally, NCHS also has provider-based surveys (such as the National Health Care Survey), population-based surveys (such as the National Health Interview Survey), and longitudinal surveys based on population surveys (such as the Longitudinal Study of Aging). Health data are usually published in *Vital and Health Statistics.*

Data systems (such as the National Archive of Computerized Data on Aging) are available from other agencies, such as the National Institute on Aging. The Centers for Disease Control publishes the *Morbidity and Mortality Weekly Report* (*MMWR*), which is available by subscription from the U.S. Government Printing Office. The statistics in the *MMWR* are based on weekly reports to the CDC by state health departments. Statistical data are also available to evaluators from state and local (city, county) health departments. The best way to get information about the content and availability of public use data tapes is to contact the agency and ask about the technical requirements and costs. Books describing the agencies are available in libraries. The U.S. Government Printing Office can be contacted directly for more information on printed reports and tables.

8. PERFORMANCE TESTS: THE "STANDARDIZED PATIENT"

Performance tests aim to measure a participants' ability to perform a specific task, such as preparing a slide for a microscope, delivering cardio-pulmonary resuscitation (CPR), or conducting an interview over the tele-phone. One technique that is unique to the health care field uses standardized patients to observe and measure the skills and behaviors required of physi-cians. The patients may be real (that is, they have the disorder or problem to be studied) or they can be actors. Extensive training and monitoring is necessary to ensure consistent adherence to the scripts. These are usually prepared by clinical experts and educators.

Standardized patients are considered by many educators to be an invalu-able tool for educating physicians and evaluating medical education. Many argue that the costs of preparing the scripts, training the patients, monitoring patient performance over time, maintaining a sufficiently large cadre of patients, and updating clinical concepts are more than offset by the value of the method in teaching and assessing clinical skills.

9. CLINICAL SCENARIOS

Clinical scenarios are particularly useful in collecting data on "what if" situations. Example 5.3 is taken from a study of physicians' attitudes toward using deception to resolve difficult ethical problems:

Example 5.3: Sample Clinical Scenarios

You are seeing Mrs. Lewis, a 52-year-old patient of yours for her annual physical, which reveals no abnormalities. You tell her that everything looks normal and that you are going to order routine blood tests and her annual screening mammography, saying that the last time you ordered it she had to pay for it herself. You know she is of modest means and cannot easily afford it. You are surprised that her health insurance does not cover it. Upon asking your secretary, you learn that insurance covers the cost of mam-mography only if there is a breast mass or objective clinical evidence of the possibility of cancer. The secretary tells you that the way to get around this is to put down "rule out cancer" instead of screening mammogra-phy on the form.

1. How would you fill out the form?

   a. Rule out cancer
   b. Screening mammography

2. If you chose (a) to question 1, was it be-cause (choose one, or rank your choices):

   a. You think the insurance company's distinctions are unreasonable.
   b. You feel a stronger obligation to your patient than to the insurance company.
   c. You feel that everyone else does it.
   d. You feel the financial hardship on Mrs. Lewis would be greater than on the insurance company.
   e. Other (please explain).

$\longrightarrow$

Example 5.3 (Continued)

3. Again, if you chose (a) to question 1, do you feel you deceived the insurance company? (Y/N)

4. If you chose (b) to question 1, was it because (choose one, or rank your choices):

    a. You think the insurance company's distinctions are reasonable.

    b. It is wrong to deceive a third party for a patient's benefit.

    c. You are worried about the legal/ professional liability involved.

    d. You feel such practices are responsible for increased health care costs.

    e. Other (please explain).

The text of this example is from D. H. Novack, B. J. Detering, R. Arnold, L. Forrow, M. Ladinsky, and J. C. Pezzullo. (1989). Physicians' attitudes toward using deception to resolve difficult ethical problems. *Journal of the American Medical Association, 261,* 2980-2985. Copyright 1981, 1991, 1992, American Medical Association; reprinted with permission.

The preparation of clinical scenarios requires great skill in writing and test construction, and the evaluator cannot be certain of the accuracy of the responses.

10. THE LITERATURE

Evaluators use the literature for reasons that range from gathering ideas for research designs and data collection and analysis methods to comparing data and conclusions across research. **The literature** is a term that is used to mean published and unpublished reports of studies or statistical findings. Published reports are often easier to locate (because published reports are in books and journals that are accessible in libraries). Because they have the advantage of public scrutiny, their authors' methods (and conclusions) may be more dependable. Publication may be in a peer-reviewed journal, a book, or a report or monograph produced by local, state, or national agencies. The following are reasons for using the literature in program evaluations.

Reasons for Evaluators' Use of the Literature

1. To set standards. The literature can provide information on the past performance of programs and populations. These may serve as a yardstick in planning an evaluation and in comparing the findings of one that has already been completed.

2. *To define variables.* The literature is a primary source of information about the ways others have defined and measured commonly used key health care variables like child abuse and neglect; high-risk behaviors; comorbid conditions; social, physical, and emotional functioning; quality of care; and quality of life.

3. *To determine sample size.* Power calculations, used to arrive at sample sizes that are large enough to reveal true differences (if they exist), require an estimation of the variance—a measure of dispersion—in the sample or population. Sometimes, however, evaluators have no readily available data on the variance in the sample of interest. The evaluator can conduct a pilot study to obtain the data. Appropriate data may be available in the literature, however, enabling the evaluator to build upon and expand the work of others.

4. *To obtain examples of designs, measures, and ways of analyzing and presenting data.* The literature can be used as a source for obtaining sound information on research methods and data collection, analysis, and reporting techniques.

5. *To determine the significance of the evaluation and of its findings.* The literature is often used to justify the need for the program and for the evaluation questions. It is also used to show whether the evaluation's findings confirm or contradict the results of other studies and to identify areas in which little or no knowledge is currently available.

6. *To conduct meta-analyses.* Meta-analyses are techniques for pooling the results of randomized controlled trials. The idea is to combine the results of smaller, more local studies to increase the power of the findings. Meta-analyses have been used to combine and evaluate tests of treatments for heart attack and breast cancer. Their use is predicated on data from experimental studies. Given that not all experiments are of equal quality, understanding how to review and interpret the literature is an important first step in conducting a meta-analysis. Very few program evaluations are randomized controlled trials, and so this technique has not been used often. Evaluations are becoming more sophisticated, so perhaps meta-analyses will be more appropriate and common in the near future.

A six-step guide to reviewing the literature is on pages 100-106.

Guidelines for Reviewing the Literature

1. Assemble the literature.

A number of computerized, bibliographic data bases are available for health program evaluators. A commonly used one is MEDLINE, the computerized data base of the National Library of Medicine. You can get to MEDLINE by doing on-line searches, using special software (like GRATEFUL MED, which is available through the National Technical Information Service), and contracting with vendors such as BRS Colleague and Dialog. Another useful data base is PSYCHINFO, which includes citations from the literature of psychology and the social sciences. Other, more specialized electronic data bases available through the National Library of Medicine include AIDSLINE, HEALTHLINE, TOXLINE, AVLINE, and ENVIROLINE.

The key to an efficient literature search is specificity. If you want all articles published by Jones between 1980 and 1993 in English about evaluations of the quality of care in U.S. teaching hospitals, you are much more likely to get what you want than if you ask for all published evaluations of quality of care in U.S. teaching hospitals. If Jones has published articles about evaluations in U.S. teaching hospitals that have appeared in the education, public policy, or social science literature, then certain articles may not turn up if you rely solely on a computerized search of one data base. For a more comprehensive search, you should investigate all potentially relevant data bases, scrutinize the references in key articles, and ask experts in the field to recommend references and bibliographic data bases.

The search itself requires careful specification of the variables and populations of concern. A first step is to decide on specific criteria for a study's inclusion into and exclusion from the literature review. Once these criteria are established, the terms used to describe them can be employed to guide the search. These are called **search terms.**

2. Identify inclusion and exclusion criteria.

These are the criteria for deciding if a study is appropriate or inappropriate for review. These criteria usually include attention to the variables and populations of concern, where and when the study was published, and its methodological quality, as can be seen in the following example of the inclusion and exclusion criteria for a review of the effectiveness of prenatal care programs.

Example 5.4: Illustrative Inclusion and Exclusion Criteria for a Review of Evaluated Prenatal Care Programs

We included evaluations of programs aiming to integrate medical and social services to improve the health outcomes of mothers and newborns. We selected only published evaluations because the editorial review process screens out the poorest studies. We chose 1980 as a starting point so that we would have a decade's data reflecting the increased accessibility to prenatal care begun by the federal government in the 1960s and 1970s. We excluded research that was primarily medical (e.g., aggressive treatment of preterm births) or psychosocial (e.g., improving mothers' self-esteem) and whose focus was on the organization of the medical care system (e.g., centralizing a region's prenatal care).

With these inclusion and exclusion criteria as guides, the evaluator can now focus on a search for studies published from 1980 forward and in all languages. The search terms will probably include "program evaluation," "prenatal care," and "health outcomes."

The following are examples of terms that were used to search the literature in two studies. The first search compared the literature (randomized, controlled trials only) to experts' recommendations for treating myocardial infarction (heart attack), and the second reviewed the efficacy of treatments for posttraumatic stress disorder (PTSD; including victims of rape, combat veterans, torture victims, and the tragically bereaved).

Example 5.5: Search Terms for Electronic Bibliographic Data Bases

1. The literature on treatments for myocardial infarction: myocardial infarction, clinical trials, multicenter studies, double-blind method, meta-analysis, and the text word "random"

2. Posttraumatic stress disorder: traumatic stress, treatment, psychotherapy, flooding, PTSD, behavior therapy, pharmacotherapy, drugs, and cognitive therapy

→

3. Select the literature.

After the articles are assembled, they usually need to be screened for irrelevant material. Because few searches (and searchers) are perfect, studies are invariably obtained that do not address the topic or that are methodologically unsound.

Screens often consist of methodological criteria. For example, articles may be screened out because they do not have a control group, data come from unreliable sources, insufficient data are presented on some important variable, or the study's findings are preliminary.

4. Identify the "best" literature.

Regardless of the scope of the literature review, a method must be employed that distinguishes among articles with differing levels of quality. Selecting the best literature means finding the most methodologically rigorous studies.

At least two individuals are needed to make an adequate appraisal of a study's quality. These individuals should be given a definition of the parameters of quality and trained to use them. Before the formal review, they should test out their understanding of the system by collaborating on one to ten articles. A third, knowledgeable person can act as adjudicator in cases of disagreement.

Figure 5.4 is an example of a set of methodological features and definitions that were used to appraise the quality of the published literature on prenatal care program evaluations.

Criteria for Selecting the Best Literature
Description of the experimental program is clear (data were given on program's duration, funding-level, services, providers, patients, standardization across sites, and so on).
Participants are randomly selected into the evaluation (all patients were selected or a random sampling).
Participants are randomly assigned to groups.
The data are collected prospectively.
Data that are collected for the evaluation are demonstrated to be valid for all main variables.
Evaluation focuses on outcomes (e.g., birth weight, gestational age, drug status of mother and baby).
Evaluation collects more than one measurement after participants complete the program.
Statistical information is sufficient to determine clinical and practical significance of the findings (e.g, confidence intervals, exact p-values, etc.).

Figure 5.4. Rating Methodological Features of the Literature: Identifying the Best Published Prenatal Care Program Evaluations

The evaluator can decide that, to be categorized as "best," a study must meet all the criteria or some fraction (a score of more than 5 of 8) or achieve certain minimum criteria (such as random assignment and valid data collection). Needless to say, these choices are somewhat arbitrary, and their merits must be defended on a case-by-case basis.

An important component of the process of deciding on a study's quality is agreement among reviewers. To identify the extent of agreement, each item in the review can be examined independently or reviewers' scores on the entire set of items can be compared.

When two or more persons measure the same item and their measurements are compared, an index of interrater reliability is obtained. One statistic that is often used in deciding on the degree of agreement among two reviewers on a dichotomous variable (valid data were collected: yes or no) is kappa (k). The statistic used to examine the relationship between two numerical characteristics (Reviewer A's score of 5 versus Reviewer B's score of 7 points) is correlation.

Not all literature reviews are done by two or more persons. Then, intra*rater reliability can be calculated using kappa or correlation. To do this, a single reviewer should rate or score a selection of articles at least twice and compare the results.

5. Abstract the information.

The most efficient way to get data from the literature is to standardize the abstraction process. A uniform abstraction system guards against the possibility that some important information will be missed, ignored, or misinterpreted. To obtain information on a study's data collection, a form like the following in Figure 5.5 is useful:

SECTION IV: Methods (continued)

Data Sources:

A. Methods:
  (check all that apply)

[ ] Direct observation   [ ] Vital statistics
[ ] Medical record review   [ ] Self-administered questionnaire
[ ] Telephone survey   [ ] Billing records
[ ] Face-to-face interview   [ ] Administrative records
[ ] Literature review   [ ] Other, specify:
                              _____

Figure 5.5. Excerpts From a Form for Obtaining Information on a Study's Data Collection

→

B. Variables measured:
(check all that apply)

[ ] Age
[ ] Race/ethnicity
[ ] Number of red cells ordered
[ ] Perioperative hemoglobin (g/dl)
Type of surgery
[ ] Orthopedic
[ ] Cardiac
[ ] General
[ ] Obstetric-gynecologic
[ ] Urology
[ ] Vascular
[ ] Thoracic
[ ] Plastic
[ ] Oral
[ ] Other

_____

C. Reliability/Validity:

1. Is any information regarding the **reliability** of selected forms, surveys, or other data collection methods discussed?

    [ ] YES---->If YES, specify (e.g., Cronbach's alpha, Kuder-Richardson, etc.):
    _____

    [ ] NO/CANNOT TELL

2. Is any information regarding the **validity** of study design, data collection or findings discussed?

    [ ] YES---->If YES, specify (e.g., used previously validated forms, reported validation studies, etc.):
    _____

    [ ] NO/CANNOT TELL

3. Are data collection procedures **standardized**? *(check all that apply)*

    [ ] YES
    [ ] NO/CANNOT TELL

D. Duration of Data Collection Period: ___ ___ months *(convert all periods to months and sum if >1 period)*

Years of Data Collection Period: 19 ___ ___ to 19 ___ ___

Figure 5.5. (Continued)

Suppose you wanted to abstract information on the characteristics of the programs that were being evaluated, you might collect information using a form such as the one on page 105.

Programs / Interventions

Program/Site combinations *(check one):*
        [ ] One program, one site (GO TO **A**)
        [ ] One program, several sites (GO TO **B**)
        [ ] Multifaceted program, one site (GO TO **C**)
        [ ] Multifaceted program, several sites (GO TO **D**)

A. ONE PROGRAM / ONE SITE:

  1. Program adequately described?

     [ ] YES---------->If **YES**, provide brief synopsis of program
                description:

                   _____

                   _____

                   _____

     [ ] NO

  2. Duration of program: ___ ___ months
     (enter "99" if unknown or not reported)
     (e.g., convert 3 years to 36 months)

  3. Funding level:
     (check one)
     [ ] Not stated   [ ] $500,000 to <$1 million
     [ ] <$50,000   [ ] $1 million to <$2 million
     [ ] $50,000 to <$100,000   [ ] $2 million to <$5 million
     [ ] $100,000 to <$250,000   [ ] >$5 million
     [ ] $250,000 to <$500,000

B. ONE PROGRAM / SEVERAL SITES:

  1. Program adequately described?

     [ ] YES---------->If **YES**, provide brief synopsis of program
                 description:

                   _____

                   _____

                   _____

     [ ] NO

  2. Duration of program: ___ ___ months
     (enter "99" if unknown or not reported)
     (e.g., convert 3 years to 36 months)

  3. Funding level:
     (check one)
     [ ] Not stated   [ ] $500,000 to <$1 million
     [ ] <$50,000   [ ] $1 million to <$2 million
     [ ] $50,000 to <$100,000   [ ] $2 million to <$5 million
     [ ] $100,000 to <$250,000   [ ] >$5 million
     [ ] $250,000 to <$500,000

  4. Number of sites: ___ ___   [ ]   CHECK HERE IF
                                 THERE ARE 100 OR
                                 MORE SITES

  5. Is the program standardized across sites?
                [ ] YES   [ ] NO   [ ] DON'T KNOW

Figure 5.6. Abstracting Program Information

6. Consider the unpublished literature.

Various analyses of the published literature have suggested the existence of a bias in favor of positive results. This means that, if a review is based solely on published articles, negative findings may be underrepresented. "Finding" unpublished articles (e.g., in someone's file drawer), however, is not an easy task. Published studies have been reviewed by experts, peers, and colleagues, and probably the most unreliable have been screened out. Nevertheless, when interpreting the findings from the published literature, the evaluator should consider the potential biases that may exist because unpublished articles are excluded.

SUMMARY AND TRANSITION TO THE NEXT CHAPTER ON EVALUATION MEASURES

This chapter explained the factors that should be taken into account when deciding on a measure or source of data for an evaluation. First, the evaluation question must be carefully reviewed so that all variables are known and clarified. Then the evaluator should consider the possible measures that are likely to provide information on each variable. Among the possibilities are self-administered questionnaires, tests of achievement and performance (e.g., clinical scenarios and the standardized patient), medical record reviews, observations and interviews, physical examinations, and statistical records. Each has advantages and limitations. For example, interviews enable the evaluator to question program participants in a relatively in-depth manner, but they can be time-consuming and financially costly. Self-administered questionnaires may be less time-consuming and costly, but they lack the intimacy of interviews, and the evaluator must always worry about the rate of responses. In selecting a source of data, look first at the evaluation question and decide if you have the technical and financial resources and the time to develop your own measure; if not, you must consider adopting or adapting an already existing measure. You must also consider the credibility to participants and consumers of whatever data source you choose. Remember to consult the literature whenever possible to identify what is available and where the current evaluation fits into the larger scheme of things.

The next chapter discusses the concepts of reliability and validity. **Reliability** refers to the consistency of the information from each source, and **validity** refers to its accuracy. The chapter also discusses the steps required in developing and validating your own measure as well as outlining the activities involved in selecting a measure that has been developed by other evaluators. Among the issues reviewed in the next chapter is "coding," that is, making sure that your measure is properly formatted or described from the point of view of the person who will enter the data into the computer. Another important issue is making sure that the components of the evaluation are logically linked. The Measurement Chart helps to portray the logical connections among the evaluation's variables and measures.

EXERCISE: COLLECTING INFORMATION: THE RIGHT DATA SOURCES

Directions

Match the descriptions and measures.

Descriptions	Measures
1. Require excellent writing skills	A. Self-administered questionnaires
2. May alter the experimental environment	B. Medical record reviews
3. Inexpensive, but may not get responses to all questions	C. Clinical scenarios
4. May measure what you know but does not measure what you can do	D. Literature
5. Not intrusive but may not contain much psychosocial information	E. Vital statistics
6. Particularly useful in the standard-setting process	F. Achievement tests
7. Must be careful that the data apply to your program	G. Observations

Suggested Readings

Antman, E. M., Lau, J., Kupelnick, B., Mosteller, F., & Chalmers, T. C. (1992). A comparison of results of meta-analyses of randomized control trials and recommendations of clinical experts: Treatments for myocardial infarction. *Journal of the American Medical Association, 268,* 240-248.

> In the methods section, the authors, who are among the most knowledgeable in the world, discuss many of the issues involved in literature reviews and cumulative meta-analyses.

Fink, A., Brook, R. H., Kosecoff, J., et al. (1987). Sufficiency of the literature on the appropriate uses of six medical and surgical procedures. *Western Journal of Medicine, 147,* 609-614.

> Useful examples of ways to describe the quality of the literature and summarize the findings.

Fink, A., & McCloskey, L. (1990). Moving child abuse and neglect prevention programs forward: Improving program evaluations. *Child Abuse & Neglect, 14,* 187-206.

> Tables and criteria for determining quality of the literature can be used as paradigms.

Fink, A., Yano, B., & Brook, R. H. (1989). The condition of the literature on hospital care and mortality. *Medical Care, 27,* 315-335.

> Describes inclusion and exclusion criteria and describes the quality of the literature. Tables are useful as prototypes for others who are interested in reviewing the literature.

Kosecoff, J., & Fink, A. (1982). *Evaluation basics.* Beverly Hills, CA: Sage.

> Contains descriptions of various sources of data used in evaluations of programs in health, education, and social welfare; provides rules for writing multiple-choice and other types of questions.

National Technical Information Service. (1985). *The basics of searching MEDLINE: A guide for the health professional.* Springfield, VA: National Library of Medicine.

> Explains the logic behind MEDLINE and describes the MeSH headings (medical subject headings). An easy-to-use guide for the serious literature reviewer.

Solomon, S. D., Gerrity, E. T., & Muff, A. M. (1992). Efficacy of treatments for posttraumatic disorder: An empirical review. *Journal of the American Medical Association, 268,* 633-638.

> Provides a useful way of summarizing the results of literature reviews that are not appropriate for meta-analyses.

U.S. Government Printing Office. (1989). *Vital and health statistics* (series). Washington, DC: Author.

The National Center for Health Statistics has data on a wide variety of health issues, such as mortality, natality, marriage, divorce, health, nutrition, and so on. This publication describes the data that are available, the specific variables, and how the data were collected. It also tells how to obtain data tapes and samples of the questionnaires and other methodological details.

Purpose of This Chapter

This chapter starts with the concepts of reliability and validity. **Reliability** refers to the consistency of a measure, and **validity** refers to its accuracy. Reliable and valid measures are the key to a sound evaluation because they are indicators of the quality upon which findings and conclusions are based. This chapter also discusses how to develop and select valid measures, prepare a coding strip for data entry, and use the Measurement Chart to establish logical connections among the evaluation's questions, design, and measures.

6 Evaluation Measures

Reliability and Validity

Evaluators sometimes create their own measures, and sometimes they adapt or adopt parts or all of already existing ones. Because the conclusions of an evaluation are based on data from these measures, their quality must be demonstrably high for the evaluation's results to be sound. (Otherwise, we have the well-known phenomenon of "garbage in-garbage out.") Determining the quality of the data collection measures means understanding their reliability and validity.

RELIABILITY

A reliable measure is one that is relatively free from "measurement error." Because of this "error," individuals' obtained scores are different than their true scores (which can only be obtained from perfect measures). What causes this error? In some cases, the error results from the measure itself: It may be difficult to understand or poorly administered. For example, a self-administered questionnaire regarding the value of preventive health care might produce unreliable results if its reading level is too high for the teen mothers who are to use it. If the reading level is on target, but the directions are unclear, the measure will be unreliable. Of course, the evaluator could simplify the language and clarify the directions and still find measurement error. This is because measurement error can also come directly from the examinees. For example, if teen mothers are asked to complete a questionnaire, and they are especially anxious or fatigued, their obtained scores could differ from their true scores.

In program evaluation, four kinds of reliability are often discussed: stability, equivalence, homogeneity, and inter- and intrarater reliability.

Stability is sometimes called "test-retest reliability." A measure is stable if the correlation between scores from time to time is high. Suppose a survey of patient satisfaction were administered to the same group of patients at Hospital A in April and again in October. If the survey were reliable, and no special program or intervention were introduced, on average, we would expect satisfaction to remain the same. The major conceptual difficulty in establishing test-retest reliability is in determining how much time is permissible between the first and second administrations. If too much time elapses, external events might influence responses for the second administration; if too little time passes, the respondents may remember and simply repeat their answers from the first administration.

Equivalence, or "alternate-form reliability," refers to the extent to which two assessments measure the same concepts at the same level of difficulty. Suppose students were given an achievement test before participating in a course and then again 2 months after completing it. Unless the evaluator were certain that the two tests were of equal difficulty, better performance after the second administration could represent performance on an easier test rather than improved learning. Because this approach to reliability requires two administrations, however, the evaluator must worry about the appropriate interval between them.

As an alternative to establishing equivalence between two forms of the same instrument, evaluators sometimes compute a split-half reliability. To do this requires dividing an instrument into two equal halves (or alternate forms) and obtaining the correlation between the two halves. Problems arise if the two halves vary in difficulty; however, because only one administration is required, at least the concern over the duration of intervals between testing is eliminated.

Homogeneity refers to the extent to which all the items or questions assess the same skill, characteristic, or quality. Sometimes this type of reliability is referred to as "internal consistency." A Cronbach's coefficient alpha, which is basically the average of all the correlations between each item and the total score, is often calculated to determine the extent of homogeneity. For example, suppose an evaluator created a questionnaire to find out about patients' satisfaction with Hospital A. An analysis of homogeneity will tell the extent to which all items on the questionnaire focus on satisfaction.

Some variables do not have a single dimension. Patient satisfaction, for example, may consist of satisfaction with nurses, doctors, financial arrangements, quality of care, quality of surroundings, and so on. If you are unsure of the number of dimensions included in an instrument, a factor analysis can be performed. This statistical procedure identifies "factors" or relationships among the items or questions.

Interrater reliability refers to the extent to which two or more individuals agree. Suppose two individuals were sent to a prenatal care clinic to observe waiting times, the appearance of the waiting and examination rooms, and the general atmosphere. If the observers agreed perfectly on all items, then interrater reliability would be perfect. Interrater reliability is enhanced by training data collectors, providing them with a guide for recording their observations, monitoring the quality of the data collection over time to see that people are not "burning out," and offering a chance to discuss difficult issues or problems.

Intrarater reliability refers to a single individual's consistency of measurement, and this, too, can be enhanced by training, monitoring, and continuous education.

VALIDITY

Validity refers to the degree to which a measure assesses what it purports to measure. For example, a test that asks students to recall information would be considered an invalid measure of their ability to apply information. Similarly, a survey of patient satisfaction will not be considered valid unless you can prove that people who are identified as satisfied on the basis of their responses to the survey think or behave differently than people who are identified as dissatisfied.

Content validity refers to the extent to which a measure thoroughly and appropriately assesses the skills or characteristics it is intended to measure. For example, an evaluator who is interested in developing a measure of quality of life for cancer patients has to define quality of life and then write items that adequately include all aspects of the definition. Because of the complexity of the task, the literature is often consulted either for a model or for a conceptual framework from which a definition can be derived. A conceptual model of "quality of life" consists of the variables to include when discussing the concept in differing kinds of patients such as those with cancer, those who are depressed, those very old or very young, and so on. It is not uncommon in establishing content validity to see a statement like this one: "We used XYZ Cognitive Theory to select items on knowledge, and we adapted the ABC Role Model Paradigm for questions about social relations."

Face validity refers to how a measure appears on the surface: Does it seem to ask all the needed questions? Does it use the appropriate language and language level to do so? Face validity, unlike content validity, does not rely on established theory for support.

Criterion validity is made up two subcategories: predictive validity and concurrent validity.

Predictive validity refers to the extent to which a measure forecasts future performance. A medical school entry examination that predicts who will do well in medical school has predictive validity.

Concurrent validity is demonstrated when two assessments agree or a new measure is compared favorably with one that is already considered valid. For example, to establish the concurrent validity of a new aptitude test, the evaluator can administer the new and the validated measure to the same group of examinees and compare the scores. Or the evaluator can administer the new test to the examinees and compare the scores with experts' judgment of students' aptitude. A high correlation between the new test and the criterion measure means concurrent validity. Establishing concurrent validity is useful when a new measure is created that claims to be better (e.g., shorter, cheaper, fairer).

Construct validity is established experimentally to demonstrate that a measure distinguishes between people who do and do not have certain characteristics. For example, an evaluator who claims constructive validity for a measure of compassionate nursing care will have to prove in a scientific manner that nurses who do well on the measure are more compassionate nurses than nurses who do poorly. Construct validity is commonly established in at least two ways:

1. The evaluator hypothesizes that the new measure correlates with one or more measures of a similar characteristic (convergent validity) and does not correlate with measures of dissimilar characteristics (discriminant validity). For example, an evaluator who is validating a new quality-of-life measure might posit that it is highly correlated with another quality-of-life instrument, a measure of functioning, and a measure of health status. At the same time, the evaluator would hypothesize that the new measure does not correlate with selected measures of social desirability (the tendency to answer questions so as to present yourself in a more positive light) or measures of hostility.

2. The evaluator hypothesizes that the measure can distinguish one group from the other on some important variable. For example, a measure of compassion should be able to demonstrate that people who are high scorers are compassionate but that people who are low scorers are unfeeling. This requires translating a theory of compassionate behavior into measurable terms, identifying people who are compassionate and who are unfeeling (according to the theory), and proving that the measure consistently and correctly distinguishes between the two groups.

A Note on Language:
Data Collection Terms

The language used to discuss reliability and validity (**examinees, scores, scales, tests, measures,** and so on) comes from test theory or "psychometrics." Program evaluators often use **data source, measure, scale, test,** and **instrument** as synonyms. This is sometimes confusing, to say the least, especially because evaluators also talk about outcome measures or outcome indicators. These usually refer to a study's outcomes. The following lexicon can be helpful in sorting out data collection terms.

A Guide to Data Collection Terms

Data source: Any source of information for the evaluation. This may include measures such as questionnaires or tests, data bases such as Medicare data tapes, epidemiological data, and vital statistics.

Index: A way of rank ordering things. Scores on an index of function give an indication of where people stand in relation to one another. Sometimes used interchangeably with **scale.**

Instrument: A synonym for **measure.** A device or strategy used to collect data including laboratory tests, self-administered questionnaires, and interviews.

Measure: Very much like data source. Sometimes called **instrument, test,** or **assessment.**

Outcome: The consequences of participating in a program such as health status or emotional well-being.

Outcome measure or outcome indicator: Often used as a synonym for **outcome.**

Rating scale: A graded set of choices. These include nominal or categorical scales (race, gender); ordered or ordinal scales ("often," "sometimes," "never"; Stage I, II, and III of a disease); numerical scales, including continuous (age, height) and discrete (number of pregnancies, number of arrests for driving drunk). A most commonly used rating scale is the Likert scale, with categories such as "strongly agree," "agree," "disagree," and "strongly disagree."

Scale: A combination of items or questions that measure the same concept, such as a 10-item scale that measures emotional well-being or a 36-item scale that measures health status.

Test: Achievement test, laboratory test.

Checklist for Creating a New Measure

Knowing the types of measures that are available and how to demonstrate reliability and validity enables evaluators to get down to the serious business of developing a measure that is tailored to the needs of their investigation or selecting and adapting one that is already in use. To create a new measure, make sure you have identified the domain of content (through observation or with the help of experts, research, and theory) and have the expertise, time, and money to complete the task. The following is a checklist of the basic steps in creating a new measure.

_____   1. **Set boundaries.**

     ____ *Decide on the type of measure* (e.g., questionnaire, observation).

     ____ *Determine the amount of needed and available time for administration and scoring* (e.g., a 15-minute interview, with 10 minutes for summarizing responses).

     ____ *Select the kinds of reliability and validity information to collect* (e.g, "alternate form reliability" means developing two forms; "concurrent validity" means availability of an already existing instrument).

_____   2. **Define the subject matter or topics that will be covered.** For definitions, consult the literature, experts, or health care consumers. For example, in an evaluation of prenatal care programs, the definitions in Example 6.1 were found in the literature and corroborated by nurses, physicians, and evaluators.

Example 6.1: Defining Terms: The Case of Prenatal Care Programs

Prenatal health care refers to pregnancy-related services provided between conception and delivery and consists of monitoring the health status of the woman; providing patient information to foster optimal health, good dietary habits, and proper hygiene; and providing appropriate psychological and social support. **Programs** have preset, specific purposes and activities for defined populations and groups. **Outcomes of prenatal care programs** include the newborn's gestational age and birth weight and the mother's medical condition and health habits.

These definitions tell the evaluator something like the following: If you want to evaluate prenatal care programs, your measures should include attention to patient education, dietary habits and hygiene, and psychosocial support. If you are interested in outcomes, you will need measures of gestational age and mother's medical condition and health habits. You will also need to decide on which medical conditions (e.g., diabetes, hypertension) and health habits (e.g, drinking, smoking) you will focus on.

_____ 3. **Outline the content.**

Suppose an evaluation were concerned with the outcomes of a prenatal care program: the Prenatal Care Access and Utilization Initiative. Assume also that a review of the literature and consultation with experts reveal the importance of collecting data on the following variables: still or live birth, birth weight, gestational age, number of prenatal visits, and drug toxicology status of mother and baby. An outline of the contents might look like this:

Outline of the Contents of a Measure of Outcomes: The Case of a Prenatal Care Program

    I. Baby's birth date
   II. Birth weight
  III. Gender
  IV. Gestational age
   V. Whether a drug toxicology screen was performed on baby and results
  VI. Whether a drug toxicology screen was performed on mother and results
 VII. Number of visits

_____ 4. **Select item choices.**

The "item" refers to the questions asked of respondents or the statements to which they are to react. Here is an example:

Item Choices: An Example

Item: What are the test results?	**Circle One**
Choices:	
Normal or negative.	1
Not significant but abnormal.	2
Positive.	3
Equivocal/No Data.	9

Selecting choices for items requires skill and practice. Whenever possible, use item choices that others have used effectively. The possibilities of finding appropriate choices are greater when collecting demographic information (e.g., age, gender, ethnicity, income, education, where a person lives), for example, than when collecting data on the knowledge, attitudes, or behaviors that are to result from a specific program designed for a particular group of people. Effective choices can be found in the published and unpublished literature and can be obtained from measures prepared by the U.S. Bureau of the Census, the health departments of cities, counties, and states, and other public and private agencies.

_____ 5. **Choose rating scales.**

These should be adapted from other, proven scales, whenever possible. Like the choices for an item, they too can come from measures designed by public and private agencies and those described in the literature. In the following item, a simple true-and-false scale is used.

Rating Scale: True-False Example

Please circle the number that **best** describes whether **each** of the following statements is true or false for you.

	1. Definitely True	2. Mostly True	3. Not sure	4. Mostly False	5. Definite- ly False
I am somewhat ill	1	2	3	4	5
I am as healthy as anybody I know	1	2	3	4	5
My health is excellent	1	2	3	4	5
I have been feeling bad lately	1	2	3	4	5

_____ 6. **Review the measure with experts and potential users.**

Reviews by other evaluators or subject matter experts and potential users are recommended. The following are questions to ask them.

Questions to Ask in Reviewing Measures

Ask Experts:

1. Is all relevant content covered?
2. Is the content covered in adequate depth?
3. Are all item choices appropriate?
4. Are all rating scales appropriate?
5. Is the measure too long?

Ask Users:

1. Is all relevant content covered?
2. Is the content covered in adequate depth?
3. Do you understand without ambiguity all item choices and scales?
4. Did you have enough time to complete the measure?
5. Did you have enough time to administer the measure?
6. Is the measure too long?

_____ 7. **Revise the measure, based on comments.**

_____ 8. **Add a "coding" strip.**

Coding the measure tells the person who enters the data into the computer into which "column" or space to put a respondent's reply. You can put the coding strip directly on the measure, as long as it does not clutter the format of the measure. Typical strips are given in Example 6.2.

Example 6.2: Example of Coding Strips

A. During the past 7 days, how many times did you eat broccoli?

   1. Once   *20*   3. Four or more
   2. Two or three times   4. I did not eat any broccoli

B. In the last week, did you eat any of the following: **Circle one for each choice of food.**

**CIRCLE
ONE**

	1. Yes	2. No	
Broccoli	1	2	*20*
Hamburger	1	2	*21*
Chicken	1	2	*22*
Spinach	1	2	*23*
Potatoes	1	2	*24*

Or

Example 6.2: (Continued)

C. Which of these did you eat in the last week? *(Check all that apply)*

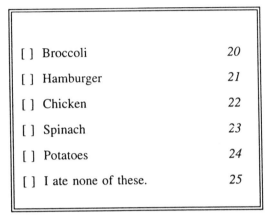

[ ] Broccoli	*20*
[ ] Hamburger	*21*
[ ] Chicken	*22*
[ ] Spinach	*23*
[ ] Potatoes	*24*
[ ] I ate none of these.	*25*

The numbers to the right of the item are the "columns" or places for recording the responses to each item. To the data enterer, it works this way:

What the Data Enterer Does for Items A, B, and C

Item A: In column 20, place a 1, 2, 3, or 4 (depending upon the person's response).

Item B: In columns 21, 22, 23, and 24, place a 1 or 2, depending on the person's response.

Item C: In columns 20, 21, 22, 23, and 24, place a 1 if checked; place a 2 if not checked.

If an item is left blank, the column must be assigned some number such as 9 (assuming eight or fewer choices). If nine choices or more, can you use another code, say, 99? The answer is yes, but then you must provide for data entry into two columns, and the numbers would be entered as 01, 02, . . . 99. Example 6.3 illustrates coding strips for items with more than nine choices or a double-digit answer.

Example 6.3: Coding Strips for Item With More Than Nine Choices or With a Double-Digit Answer

D. What was your **total** household **income before taxes** in 1993?

[ ]	$10,000 or less	*20-21*
[ ]	$10,100 to $12,000	
[ ]	$12,100 to $15,000	
[ ]	$15,100 to $20,000	
[ ]	$21,000 to $30,000	
[ ]	$31,000 to $40,000	
[ ]	$41,000 to $50,000	
[ ]	$51,000 to $70,000	
[ ]	$71,000 to $90,000	
[ ]	Over $90,000	

E. How many people in your household are supported by your total household income?

_____   _____   *50 - 51*

_____ 9. **Check the numbering and coding of skip patterns**. A *skip pattern* refers to one or more items that a respondent does not have to complete because the items are not pertinent:

Coding Strip for an Item with a Skip Pattern

Have you ever been told to stop smoking by a doctor, nurse, or other health care professional?

1	[ ] NO--->	**Go to question 8**	*21*
2	[ ] YES--->	Did you stop smoking?	
		1 [ ] yes	*22*
		2 [ ] no	

As a rule, skip patterns should be used only with skilled observers and interviewers. Avoid skip patterns in self-administered surveys.

_____ 10. **Put the measure in an appropriate format;** for example:

  ___ Add an ID code because without it you cannot collect data on the same person over time.

  ___ Add directions for administration and completion.

  ___ Add a statement regarding confidentiality (meaning that persons are identifiable by code) or anonymity (no means of identification).

  ___ Thank the respondent.

  ___ Give instructions for submitting the completed measure. If mailed, is an addressed and stamped envelope provided? By what date should the measure be completed?

_____ 11. **The measure should be reviewed and tested before administration.**

The importance of pilot testing a new measure cannot be over emphasized. A pilot test requires using the measure in realistic conditions. This means using the measure with as many participants as the evaluation's resources will allow. After they have completed the measure, interview the participants to find out about the problems they might have had. With interviews, the methods for interviewing as well answering the questions should be tested.

Checklist for Selecting an Already Existing Measure

Many instruments and measures are available for use by health program evaluators. A good source for them is the published evaluations found in journals. In some cases, the whole instrument is published as part of the article. But, if not, the "methods" section usually describes all main data sources and measures, and the evaluator can contact the authors for additional information.

Using an already tested measure has many advantages. Among them is the hope of saving time and other resources needed to develop and validate a completely new instrument. Choosing a measure that has been used elsewhere is not without pitfalls, however. You may be required to pay for the measure, you may have to share your data, or you may have to substantially modify the measure so that its reliability and validity are jeopardized, requiring you to establish them all over again.

The following is a checklist for choosing an already existing measure.

_____ 1. **Find out the costs:** Do you have to pay? Share data? Share authorship?

_____ 2. **Check the content:** In essence, you must do your own face- and content-validity study. Make sure that the questions are the ones you would ask if you were developing the instrument. Check the choices and rating scales. Will they get you the information you need?

_____ 3. **Check the reliability and validity:** Check to see that the types of reliability and validity that have been confirmed are appropriate for your needs. If you are interested in interrater reliability, but only internal consistency statistics are provided, the measure may not be the right one. If you are interested in a measure's ability to predict, but only content validity data are available, think again before adopting the instrument.

Check carefully the context in which the measure has been validated. Are the settings and groups similar to those in your evaluation? If not, the instrument may not be valid for your purposes. For example, a measure of compliance with counselors' advice in a program to prevent child abuse and neglect that has been tested on teen mothers in Montana may not be applicable to nonteen mothers in Helena, Montana, or to teen mothers in San Francisco, California.

The evaluator must also decide if a measure is sufficiently reliable and valid for use. Reliability and validity are often described as correlations (say, between experts or measures or among items). How high should the correlations be? The fast answer is that the higher, the better, and .90 is best. But the statistic by itself should not be the only or even the most important criterion. A lower correlation may be acceptable if the measure has other properties that are potentially more important. For example, the content may be especially appropriate or the measure might have been tested on participants who are very much like those in the current evaluation.

_____ 4. **Check the measure's format:**

- Will the data collectors be able to score the measure?
- Does it make sense to use it, given your available technology? For example, if it requires certain software or expertise, do you have it? Can you afford to get it?
- Will the participants in the evaluation be willing to complete the measure? Participants sometimes object to spending more than 10 or 15 minutes on an interview, for example. Also, personal questions and complicated instructions can result in incomplete data.

The Measurement Chart: Logical Connections

A measurement chart assists the evaluator in the logistics of the evaluation by making sure that all variables will have the appropriate coverage. The chart is also useful in writing proposals because it portrays the logical connections among what is being measured, how, for how long, and with whom. When writing reports, the chart provides a summary of some of the important features of the evaluation's data sources. Look at the Measurement Chart in Table 6.1, on pages 124-125.

Table 6.1. Measurement Chart

Dependent Variables	How Measured	Sample	Timing of Measurements	Duration of Measurements	Content	Reliability and Validity	General Concerns
Quality of life	Interviews with patients	All 100 patients in the E group and all 100 in the control. In each group of 100, 50 men and 50 women	One month before program participation, one month after, and one year after	One-hour interviews, with 30 minutes to summarize	Social, emotional, and physical functioning; health beliefs; perceived joy and satisfaction: 35 questions	The Brandyse Functional Assessment (long-form) and the University Quality of Living Scale will be adopted. The Brandyse has been validated on 4,000 community-dwelling elderly. Test-retest reliability is .85 and homogeneity for subscales is .90.	No costs will be incurred; data will be shared with the Brandyse group. The University Quality of Living Scale is available free to all researchers. All patients will complete an informed consent form. No special institutional review board-type procedure need be followed. No special software or hardware is necessary.
	Observations	50 patients in the experimental and 50 in the control groups, with 25 men and 25 women	One month before program participation and six months after	Half-hour observations; 15 minutes to summarize	Appearance and repair of household; number of visitors; fire and accident safety: 10 questions	Interrater reliability will be estimated between at least two observers.	

Health status	Physical examination	All persons in experimental and control groups	One month before the program, within one month of completion and one year later	30 minutes	Emphasis on presence or absence of serious chronic disorders (e.g., metastatic cancer; heart disease): 50 questions	A team of four physicians and nurse practitioners will be trained to administer the physical examinations in a uniform way.
Demographic characteristics	Self-administered questionnaires or interviews	All persons in experimental and control groups	One month before the start of the program	Less than 5 minutes	Gender, ethnicity, age, education, household income, region of county in which highest level of education was achieved: 10 questions	Standard items will be used to collect these data.
Costs	Financial records	All persons receiving care in two clinics: one primarily staffed by physicians and one by nurses	Within one month of the completion of the program	About 30 minutes to obtain data and make calculations	Number of staff; hourly wages; number of appointments to each clinic made and kept; number of minutes spent on care	A form will be created and data collectors will be trained to use it. Periodic quality checks will be made.

Each column of the chart attempts to make logical connections among each segment of data collection.

Variables. To ensure that all independent and dependent variables are covered, check the evaluation questions and sampling strategies, including all strata and inclusion and exclusion criteria. For example, suppose an evaluation asked about the effectiveness of a year-long combined diet and exercise program in improving the health status and quality of life for people over 75 years of age. Suppose also that it excluded all persons with certain diseases such as metastatic cancer and heart disease. Assume also that men and women were to be compared to determine whether any differences existed after program participation. Then, the variables needing measurement include quality of life, health status (to identify persons with metastatic cancer and heart disease and assess changes), and demographic characteristics (to determine who is male and who is female).

How measured. For each variable, the measure should be indicated. The Measurement Chart shows that quality of life will be assessed through interviews with patients and observations of how they live; health status will be measured by physical examination; demographic characteristics, by self-administered questionnaire or interviews; and costs, through a review of financial records.

Sample. This refers to the number and characteristics of individuals who will constitute the sample for each measure. For example, to measure quality of life, the Measurement Chart shows that the evaluator will interview all 100 patients (50 men and 50 women) in the experimental group and all 100 patients (50 men and 50 women) in the control group as well as observe a sample of the life-styles of 50 patients (25 men and 25 women) in each group. To assess health status, all persons in the experimental and control groups will be examined. According to the Measurement Chart, demographic information will be collected on all experimental and control program participants. Data on costs will be collected just for those individuals who use one of the two staffing models.

Timing of measures. **Timing** refers to when each measure is to be administered. For example, the Measurement Chart shows that interviews regarding quality of life and physical examinations will be given 1 month before the program, immediately after (within 1 month), and 1 year after. Observations will be made 1 month before and 6 months after. Demographic information will be obtained just once: 1 month before the start of the program.

Duration of measures. **Duration** means the amount of time each will take to administer and summarize or score. The Measurement Chart shows that the quality-of-life interviews will take 1 hour to conduct and a half hour to summarize. The observations will take a half hour to conduct and 15 minutes to summarize. The physical examinations are expected to take 30 minutes and collecting data on demographic characteristics will take about 5 minutes.

Content. A brief description of the content should be provided in the chart. For example, if measurement of quality of life is to be based on a theory, then it should be named. If the interview has several sections (e.g., social, emotional, and physical function), they can be discussed. It should be noted that the chart is really a guide to the measurement features of an evaluation. Each one of its sections may require elaboration. For example, for some measures, you may want to include the number of items in each subscale.

Reliability and validity. If the measures being used are adapted from some other study, the relevant types of reliability and validity statistics might be described. For example, if the quality-of-life measure were used on elderly people in another evaluation that showed that higher scorers had higher quality than low scorers, this can be mentioned. If additional reliability information is to be collected in the current evaluation, that, too, can be reported. A review of medical records to provide information on the number, types, and appropriateness of admissions to the hospital over a 1-year period, for example, could require estimations of data collectors' interrater reliability; such information belongs in this section of the chart.

Other general concerns. In this portion of the chart, any special features of the entire data collection and measurement endeavor should be noted. These include costs, training, number of items, special software or hardware requirements, and issues pertaining to informed consent.

SUMMARY AND TRANSITION TO THE NEXT CHAPTER ON DATA ANALYSIS

Reliability refers to the consistency of a measure, and **validity** refers to its accuracy. Having reliable and valid measures is essential in a diligent evaluation. Sometimes the evaluator is required or chooses to create a new measure; at other times, a measure is available that appears to be suitable. Whether creating, adapting, or adopting, the evaluator must critically review the measure to ensure its appropriateness and accuracy for the current study.

The Measurement Chart is a useful way of showing the relationships among dependent variables, how and when the dependent variables are measured, and the content, reliability, and validity of the measures. The Measurement Chart can be used in planning and reporting on evaluations.

The next chapter on analysis discusses and explains the most commonly used methods of data analysis in program evaluations. To choose among them requires identifying the independent and dependent variables and understanding the nature of the evaluation's data and the measurement scales from which they are derived. The chapter also provides information on how to assess statistical and clinical significance and to use meta-analysis to combine the results of relatively small, local studies. Practical concerns, such as cleaning and transforming data and preparing a codebook with instructions for data entry, are also addressed.

EXERCISES: DATA COLLECTION

EXERCISE 1: RELIABILITY AND VALIDITY

Directions

Read the following excerpts and determine which concepts of reliability and validity are covered.

A. The self-administered questionnaire was adapted with minor revisions from the Student Health Risk Questionnaire, which is designed to investigate knowledge, attitudes, behaviors, and various other cognitive variables regarding HIV and AIDS among high school students. . . . Four behavior scales measured sexual activity (4 questions in each scale) and needle use (5 questions); 23 items determined a scale of factual knowledge regarding AIDS. Cognitive variables derived from the Health Belief Model and Social Learning Theory were employed to examine personal beliefs and social norms (12 questions).

B. All charts were reviewed by a single reviewer with expertise in this area; a subset of 35 charts was reviewed by a second blinded expert to assess the validity of the review. Rates of agreement for single items ranged from 81% ($k = .77$; $P < .001$) to 100% ($k = 1$; $P < .001$).

C. Group A and Group B nurses were given a 22-question quiz testing evaluation principles derived from the UCLA guidelines. It was not scored in a blinded manner, but each test was scored twice.

EXERCISE 2: CREATING AND CODING MEASURES

Directions

You are the evaluator of a prenatal care program. One of the evaluation questions asks about characteristics of the babies born to participating mothers. The project routinely collects data on mothers and babies, but you need data on birth weight, gestational age, whether the baby was stillborn, whether a drug toxicology screen was performed at birth on the mother and the baby (and the results), the number of prenatal care visits, and the birth date.

1. Create the form for obtaining this information.
2. Add a coding strip.

EXERCISE 3: REVIEWING A DATA COLLECTION PLAN

Directions

Read the following information collection scenario and, acting as an independent reviewer, provide the evaluator with a description of your problems and concerns.

The School of Nursing is in the process of revising its elective course in research methods. As part of the process, a survey was sent to all faculty who currently teach the methods courses to find out whether and to what extent epidemiology topics were included. Among the expectations was that methods courses would aim to improve students' knowledge of epidemiology and their attitudes toward its usefulness in a number of nursing subjects ranging from public health nursing to home health care administration. The results of the survey revealed little coverage of some important objectives. Many faculty indicated that they would like to include more epidemiology, but they were lacking educational materials and did not have the resources to prepare their own. To rectify this, a course with materials was developed and disseminated. The Center for Nursing, Education, and Evaluation was asked to appraise the effectiveness of the educational materials.

Evaluators from the center prepared a series of knowledge and skill tests and planned to administer them each year over a 5-year period. The evaluators are experts in test construction, and so they decided to omit pilot testing and save the time and expense. Their purpose in testing was to measure changes (if any) in nurses' abilities. They also planned to interview a sample of cooperating students to get an in-depth portrait of their knowledge of clinical epidemiology.

Suggested Readings

Babbie, E. B. (1992). *The practice of social research* (6th ed.). Belmont, CA: Wadsworth.

> A textbook that contains useful discussions on various evaluation topics including measurement. Criteria for measuring reliability and validity are discussed as well as how to design scales and indexes.

Ganz, P., Schag, C. A. C., Lee, J. J., & Sim, M. (1992). The CARES: A generic measure of health-related quality of life for patients with cancer. *Quality of Life Research, 1,* 19-29.

> This article describes the validation of the Cancer Rehabilitation Evaluation System (CARES). It provides an excellent example of the way in which a new measure is tested.

McDowell, I., & Newell, C. (1987). *Measuring health: A guide to rating scales and questionnaires.* New York: Oxford University Press.

> This book provides numerous examples of health measurement techniques and scales. The validity and reliability of important health measures are discussed. This book is useful for learning about reliability and validity and the types of measures and scales that are available to the health researcher.

Stewart, A. L., Hays, R. D., & Ware, J. E. (1988). The MOS short-form health survey: Reliability and validity in a patient population. *Medical Care, 26,* 724-735.

> The statistics used to establish the reliability and validity of a widely used measure of health.

Tulsky, D. S. (1990). An introduction to test theory. *Oncology, 4,* 43-48.

> Definitions and examples of the concepts of reliability and validity.

Review Notes

Purpose of This Chapter

Program evaluators use statistical methods to analyze and summarize data and to come to conclusions that can be applied to program planning and policy. The statistical methods are derived from the fields of statistics and epidemiology. **Biostatistics** refers to the application of statistics to biological and health sciences. **Epidemiology** includes the study of health and illness in human populations (not individuals). Choosing a method to analyze program evaluation data is an intellectual process in which statistical technology and the outcomes of health interventions converge. This chapter discusses key components of the intellectual process.

Specifically, this chapter addresses the associations among the evaluation questions, design, sample, and data sources and shows how the choice of analysis is as much a function of the characteristics of the evaluation questions and the quality of the data available to evaluators as it is dependent upon their ability to identify the appropriate statistical technique. The chapter does not focus on how to perform statistical operations (which is better covered in statistics texts and computer manuals) but does center on the pertinent uses of the procedures most commonly employed by health program evaluators. Because hypothesis testing, confidence intervals, and meta-analyses are particularly important topics in evaluation, they receive special attention.

7 Analyzing Evaluation Data

A Suitable Analysis:
Starting With the Evaluation Questions

To select the most suitable analysis for evaluation, the evaluator must answer these questions:

1. What independent and dependent variables are contained within each evaluation question (and its associated standard)?
2. In what form or from what kind of scale will data be provided? Data can come from nominal scales (male, female); ordinal scales (high, medium, low); and numerical scales (a score of 30 out of 100 possible points).
3. What statistical methods may be used to answer the evaluation question, given its independent and dependent variables?
4. Do the evaluation's data meet all the assumptions of the statistical tests? (For example, is the sample size sufficient? Are the data "normally distributed"?)

Measurement Scales and Their Data

A first step in selecting a statistical method is to identify the type of data resulting from each measure used to collect data on the independent and dependent variables. A variable is a characteristic that is measurable. A patient's weight is a variable, and all persons weighing 55 kilograms have the same numerical weight. A patient's satisfaction is also a variable. In this case, however, the numerical scale has to be devised and rules must be created for its interpretation. For example, in Evaluation A, patient satisfaction might be measured on a scale of 1 to 100, with 1 corresponding to the very lowest satisfaction and 100 to the very highest. In Evaluation B, patient satisfaction might be measured by counting the number of people who return each year for services, and, if the number equals a preset standard, then participants will be considered satisfied.

Independent variables are used to explain or predict a program's outcomes (or dependent variables). Typical independent variables in program evaluations include group membership (experimental and control), health status (excellent, very good, good, fair, poor), age, and other demographic and health characteristics. Typical dependent variables are "outcomes" such as health status (including physical, social, and psychological functioning), mortality, efficiency, quality of care, and learning.

Evaluators most often rely on three types of measurement scales, and these are termed **nominal, ordinal,** and **numerical.** In turn, the data they produce are called nominal, ordinal, and numerical data or variables or observations.

NOMINAL SCALES

Nominal scales produce data that fit into categories. Because of this, they are sometimes called **categorical:**

1. What is the patient's gender?	Circle one
Male.	1
Female.	2
2. Describe the type of lung cancer.	**Circle one**
Small cell.	1
Large cell.	2
Oat cell.	3
Squamous cell.	4

Both questions categorize the responses and require the answer to "name" the category into which the data fit. When nominal data take on one of two values as in the second question (e.g., the category of disease is present or absent), they are termed **dichotomous** (as in "divide").

Typically, nominal data are described as percentages and proportions (50 of 100—50%—of the sample was male). The measure used to describe the center of their distribution is the mode or the number of observations that appears most frequently.

ORDINAL SCALES

If an inherent order exists among categories, the data are said to be obtained from an ordinal scale:

How much education have you completed?	Circle one
Never finished high school.	1
High school graduate, but no college.	2
Some college.	3
College graduate.	4
Stage of Tumor	**Circle one**
Duke's A.	1
Duke's B.	2
Duke's C.	3
Duke's D.	4

Ordinal scales produce data that are used to classify diseases according to their severity. For example, colorectal tumors are classified in order, from Duke's A—in situ—to Duke's D—systemic disease. Ordinal scales typically are seen in questions that call for ratings of health (excellent, very good, good, fair, poor, very poor), agreement (strongly agree, agree, disagree, strongly disagree), and the probability that something is present (definitely present, probably present, probably not present, definitely not present).

Percentages and proportions are used with ordinal data, and the center of the distribution is often expressed as the median or the observation that divides the distribution into two halves. The median is equal to the 50th percentile.

NUMERICAL (INTERVAL AND RATIO) SCALES

When differences between numbers have a meaning on a numerical scale, they are called **numerical.** For example, age is a numerical variable, and so is weight, length of survival, birth weight, and many laboratory values. Numerical data are amenable to precision, so that the evaluator, for example, can obtain data on age to the nearest second.

Some health researchers distinguish between interval and ratio scales. Ratio scales have a true 0 point (as in the absolute zero value of the Kelvin scale). In program evaluations, however, ratio scales are extremely rare, and, statistically, interval and ratio scales are treated the same; hence the term "numerical" is a more apt (and neutral) phrase.

Numerical data can be continuous: height, weight, age. Or they may be discrete: numbers of visits to this clinic, numbers of previous pregnancies. Means and standard deviations are used to summarize the values of numerical measures.

The chart on page 137 contrasts the types of scales and data that are essential in choosing methods of analysis:

Selecting a Method of Analysis

The choice of method to use in analyzing data for each evaluation question is dependent upon the following:

- whether the independent variable is nominal, ordinal, or numerical
- the number of independent variables
- whether the dependent variable is nominal, ordinal, or numerical
- the number of dependent variables
- whether the design, sampling, and quality of the data meet the assumptions of the statistical method

Example 7.1 on page 138 shows the relationships among evaluation questions, independent and dependent variables, research design and sample, types of measures, and data analysis:

Measure-ment Scale and Type of Data	Examples	Comments
Nominal	Type of disease: small cell, large cell, oat cell, and squamous cell cancer; source of transfused blood: autologous donation, homologous donation; ethnicity; gender	Observations belong to categories. Observations have no inherent order of importance. Observations sometimes called categorical. When data assume two values (yes the disease is present or no it is not), they are termed dichotomous. Percentages and proportions are used to describe nominal data, and the mode is used to measure the midpoint.
Ordinal	Staging of disease: carcinoma of the cervix is staged from 0 to IV, where stage 0 is in situ and stage IV represents carcinoma extending beyond the pelvis; socioeconomic status	Order exists among the categories, that is, one observation is greater than the other. Percentages and proportions are used to describe ordinal data; the measure of the center of the distribution of the data is often the median.
Numerical	Continuous numerical scales: scores on a test of health status; age; height; length of survival; laboratory values such as serum glucose and sodium potassium Discrete numerical scales: number of visits to a nurse practitioner; number of falls	Differences between numbers have meaning on a numerical scale (e.g., higher scores mean better achievement than lower scores, and a difference between 12 and 13 has the same meaning as a difference between 99 and 100). Some statisticians distinguish between interval scales (arbitrary 0-point as in the Fahrenheit scale) and ratio scales (with an absolute 0 as in the Kelvin scale); in program evaluation, these measures are treated the same statistically, so they are combined here as numerical. Means and standard deviations are used to describe numerical data.

Figure 7.1. Measurement Scales: Nominal, Ordinal, and Numerical Variables

---

Example 7.1: Analyzing Evaluation Data: Illustrative Connections Among Questions, Designs, Samples, Measures, and Analysis

Evaluation question: Is quality of life satisfactory?

Standard: A statistically significant difference in quality of life favoring program versus control group participants

Independent variable: Group membership (program participants versus controls)

Design: An experimental design with concurrent controls

Sampling: Eligible participants are assigned at random to an experimental and a control group; 150 participants are in each group (a statistically derived sample size).

Dependent variable: Quality of life

Types of data: Group membership (nominal data); quality of life (numerical data from the CARES Questionnaire, a 100-point survey in which higher scores mean better quality)

Analysis: A two-sample independent groups t-test

Justification for the analysis: This t-test is appropriate when the independent variable is measured on a nominal scale and the dependent variable is measured on a numerical scale. In this case, the assumptions of a t-test are met. These assumptions are that each group has a sample size of at least 30, both groups' size is about equal, the two groups are independent (an assumption that is met most easily with a strong evaluation design and a high-quality data collection effort), and the data are normally distributed. (If one of the assumptions is seriously violated, other rigorous analytic methods should be used such as the Wilcoxon Rank-Sum Test, also called the Mann-Whitney U test. This test makes no assumption about the normality of the distribution; whereas the t is termed **parametric,** this test is one of a number called **nonparametric.)**

The classification of data into nominal, ordinal, and numerical is a guide for the program evaluator. Each evaluation and set of data will vary. For the sake of simplicity, for example, evaluators sometimes treat independent variables that are measured on an ordinal scale as if they were nominal.

Example 7.2: Some Exceptions: Taking Liberties with Nominal, Ordinal, and Numerical Data

Evaluation question: How do patients with a differing extent of illness compare in their satisfaction with the nurse-run clinics?

Independent variable: Extent of illness

Measurement scale: Ordinal: great, moderate, some; in choosing an analytic method, treat great, moderate, and some as nominal

Dependent variable: Satisfaction (with clinic)

Measurement scale: Numerical: scores on the Patient Satisfaction Survey

Analysis: One-way ANOVA (presuming the necessary assumptions are met)

Evaluation question: How do people of differing ages compare in their satisfaction with their health care?

Independent variable: Age

Measurement scale: Numerical (ratio); in choosing an analytic method, treat as nominal with only two values—under 55 years and over 55 years

Dependent variable: Numerical: scores on the Patient Satisfaction Survey

Analysis: t-test (presuming the necessary assumptions are met)

Dependent variables that are measured on an ordinal scale are treated as if they were numerical. Other exceptions exist as well. The following are examples of some of these exceptions.

Unfortunately, no definitive rules can be set for all evaluations and their data. Figure 7.2 on page 140, however, is a general guide to the selection of 15 of the most commonly used data-analytic methods. To use the guide, the evaluator must identify the number and measurement characteristics of the independent and dependent variables.

For simplicity, the guide omits ordinal variables. When independent variables are measured on an ordinal scale, they are often treated as if they were nominal. For example, an evaluation whose aim is to predict the outcomes of participation in a program for patients with good, fair, and poor functional status can regard good, fair, and poor (ordinal, independent variables) as nominal. When dependent variables are measured on an ordinal scale, they are habitually treated as if they were numerical. For example, if the dependent variable in a nutrition program is the length of time a diet is maintained (less than 3 months, between 3 and 6 months, and more than 6 months) by men and women with differing motivations to diet, the dependent, ordinal variable can, for the sake of the analysis, be regarded as numerical.

Remember to check the assumptions (in a statistics text or computer manual) before conducting any statistical analysis. If the evaluation's data do not meet the assumptions, look for other statistical methods to use. Methods in biostatistics and epidemiology are continuously advancing, and new methods may be emerging that meet the needs of a particular program evaluation.

Sample Questions	Type of Data: Independent Variable	Type of Data: Dependent Variable	Analytic Method
For questions with one independent and one dependent variable:			
Do experimental and control patients differ in their use or failure to use mental health services?	Nominal: group (experimental and control)	Nominal: use of mental health services (used services or did not)	Chi-square; Fisher's exact test; relative risk (risk ratio); odds ratio
How do the experimental and control groups compare in their attitudes (measured by their scores on the Attitude Survey)?	Nominal (dichotomous): group (experimental and control)	Numerical: attitude scores	Independent samples, *t*-test
How do teens in the U.S., Canada, and England compare in their attitudes (measured by their scores on the Attitude Survey)?	Nominal (more than two values: U.S., Canada, and England)	Numerical: attitude scores	One-way ANOVA (uses the *F*-test)
Do high scores on the Attitude Survey predict high scores on the Knowledge Test?	Numerical (attitude scores)	Numerical (knowledge scores)	Regression (when neither variable is independent or dependent, use correlation)
For questions with two or more independent variables:			
Do men and women in the experimental and control programs differ in whether or not they adhered to a diet?	Nominal (gender, group)	Nominal (adhered or did not adhere to a diet)	Log-linear
Do men and women with differing scores on the Knowledge Test differ in her or not they adhered to a diet?	Nominal (gender) and numerical (knowledge scores)	Nominal and dichotomous (adhered or did not adhere to a diet)	Logistic regression
How do men and women in the experimental and control programs compare in their attitudes (measured by their scores on the Attitude Survey)?	Nominal (gender and group)	Numerical (attitude scores)	Analysis of variance (ANOVA)
How are age and income and years living in the community related to attitudes (measured by scores on the Attitude Survey)?	Numerical (age and income and years living in the community)	Numerical (attitude scores)	Multiple regression

Figure 7.2. A General Guide to Data-Analytic Methods in Program Evaluation

Sample Questions	Type of Data: Independent Variable	Type of Data: Dependent Variable	Analytic Method
How do men and women in the experimental and control programs compare in their attitudes (measured by their scores on the Attitude Survey) when their level of education is controlled?	Nominal (gender and group) with confounding factors (such as education)	Numerical (attitude scores)	Analysis of covariance (ANCOVA)
For questions with two or more independent and dependent variables:			
How do men and women in the experimental and control programs compare in their attitude and knowledge scores?	Nominal (gender and group)	Numerical (scores on two measures: attitudes and knowledge)	Multivariate analysis of variance (MANOVA)

Figure 7.2. (Continued)

Hypothesis Testing, *P* Values, and Confidence Intervals: Statistical and Practical Significance

Evaluators often compare two or more groups to find out if differences in outcome exist that favor a program; if differences are present, the magnitude of those differences are examined for significance. Consider the following:

Example 7.2

Evaluation question: Do participants improve in their knowledge of how to interpret food-label information in making dietary choices?

Standards: 1. A statistically significant difference in knowledge between participants and nonparticipants must be found. The difference in scores must be at least 15 points.
2. If a 15-point difference is found, participants will be studied for 2 years to determine the extent to which the knowledge is retained. The scores must be maintained (no significant differences) over the 2-year period.

Measurements: Knowledge is measured on the Dietary Choices Test, a 25-item self-administered test.

Analysis: A *t*-test will be used to compare the two groups in their knowledge. Scores will be computed a second time, and a *t*-test will be used to compare the average or mean differences over time.

In Example 7.2, tests of statistical significance are called for twice: to compare participants and nonparticipants at one point in time and to compare the same participants' scores over time. In addition, the stipulation is that, for

the scores to have practical meaning, a 15-point difference between participants and nonparticipants must be obtained and sustained. With experience,
health program evaluators have found that, in a number of situations, statistical significance is sometimes insufficient evidence of a program's merit. With
very large samples, for example, very small differences in numerical values
(such as scores on an achievement test or laboratory values) can be statistically
significant but have little practical, educational, or clinical meaning and may
actually incur more costs than benefits.

In the example on page 141, the standard includes a 15-point difference
in test scores. If the difference between scores is statistically significant but
only 10 points, then the program will not be considered significant in a
practical sense.

Statistical significance and the P *value.* A statistically significant program
evaluation effect is one that is probably due to a planned intervention rather
than to some chance occurrence. To determine statistical significance, the
evaluator restates the evaluation question as a null hypothesis and sets the
level of significance and the value the test statistic must obtain to be significant. After this is completed, the calculations are performed. See the guidelines on pp. 143-145 for the steps to take in conducting a hypothesis test and
in determining statistical significance.

Practical Significance:
Using Confidence Intervals

The results of a statistical analysis may be significant, but not necessarily
practical. In clinical research, this duality is called "statistical" versus "clinical significance." The following discussion is taken from an editorial in the
Annals of Internal Medicine. (See the Suggested Readings at the end of the
chapter for the complete reference.) Although the editorial in the *Annals* refers
to the clinical significance of a treatment for cancer, the issues discussed and
the extreme clarity of the discussion make it especially useful for program
evaluators.

Evaluation 1. Suppose that, in a large, multicenter evaluation of a program in
pain management for cancer patients, 480 of 800 (60%) respond well to the
new program, while 416 of the 800 (52%) do well in the traditional or standard
program. Using a chi-square to assess the existence of a real difference
between the two treatments, a *P* value of .001 is obtained. This value is the
probability of obtaining by chance the 8-point (60%-52%) difference between
patients in the new and traditional programs or an even larger difference. The
point estimate is 8 percentage points, but because of sampling and measurement errors (they always exist in evaluation research), the estimate is probably
not identical to the true percentage difference between the two groups of

Guidelines for Hypothesis Testing, Statistical Significance, and P Values

1. State the evaluation question as a null hypothesis. The null hypothesis (H_0) is a statement that no difference exists between the averages or means of two groups. For example, typical null hypotheses in program evaluations are as follows:

- No difference exists between the experimental and the control programs' means.
- No difference exists between the sample's (the evaluation's participants) mean and the population's mean (the population from which the participants were sampled).

When evaluators find that a difference does not exist between means, the terminology used is this: "We failed to reject the null hypothesis." Do not say, "We accepted the null hypothesis." Failing to reject the null suggests that a difference probably exists between the means, say between Program A and Program B. Until the data are examined, however, you do not know if A is favored or B is. When you have no advance knowledge of which is better, you use a two-tailed hypothesis test. When you have an alternative hypothesis in mind—say, A is larger (better) than B—you use a one-tailed test. Before you can describe the properties of the test, other activities must take place.

2. State the level of significance for the statistical test (for example, the t-test) being used. The level of significance, when chosen before the test is performed, is called the alpha value (denoted by the Greek letter alpha: α). The alpha gives the probability of rejecting the null hypothesis when it is actually true. Tradition keeps the alpha value small—.05, .01, or .001—because among the last things an evaluator needs is to reject a null hypothesis when, in fact, it is true and there is no difference between group means.

The *P* value is the probability that an observed result (or result of a statistical test) is due to chance (and not to the program). It is calculated *after* the statistical test. If the *P* value is less than alpha, then the null is rejected.

→

Guidelines (Continued)

Current practice requires the specification of exact *P* values. That is, if the obtained *P* is .03, report that number rather than *P* < .05. Reporting the approximate *P* was common practice before the widespread use of computers (when statistical tables were the primary source of probabilities). The practice has not been eradicated, however. The merits of using the exact values can be seen in that, without them, a finding of *P* = .06 may be viewed as not significant, while a finding of *P* = .05 will be.

3. Determine the value the test statistic must attain to be significant. The values can be found in statistical tables. For example, for the *z* distribution (a standard, normal distribution) with an alpha of .05, and a two-tailed test, tabular values (found in practically all statistics books) will show that the area of acceptance for the null hypothesis is the central 95% of the *z* distribution and that the areas of rejection are 2.5% of the area in each tail. The value of *z* (found in statistical tables) that defines these areas is −1.96 for the lower tail and +1.96 for the upper tail. If the test statistic is less than −1.96 or greater than +1.96, it will be rejected. The areas of acceptance and rejection in a standard normal distribution using α = .05 are illustrated on page 145.

4. Perform the calculation. Numerous statistical packages are available for making statistical computations. To choose among them, the evaluator can consult computing software reviews in professional journals of statistics, epidemiology, and medicine. Another option is to ask for recommendations. Each of the packages has a manual (and/or tutorial) that teaches how to enter data and perform the calculations.

patients. A confidence interval provides a plausible range for the true value. A confidence interval is computed from sample data that have a given probability that the unknown true value is located between them. Using a standard method, the 95% confidence interval (95% CI) of the 8-percentage-point difference comes out to be between 3% and 13%. A 95% CI means that

Guidelines *(Continued)*

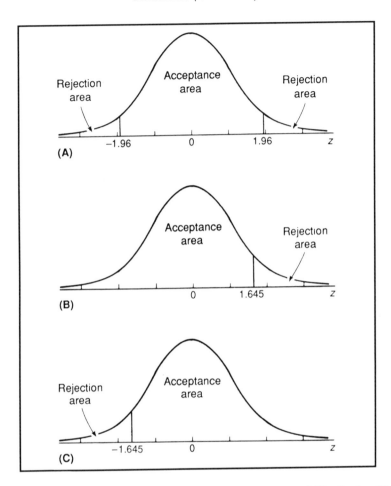

Figure 7.3. Areas of Acceptance and Rejection in a Standard Normal Distribution (Using $\alpha = .05$)

NOTE: Defining areas of acceptance and rejection in standard normal distribution using $\alpha = .05$; (A) two-tailed or non-directional; (B) one-tailed or directional upper tail; (C) one-tailed or directional lower tail.
SOURCE:B. Dawson-Saunders and R. Trapp. (1990). Basic and clinical biostatistics (New York: Appleton and Lange), p. 74; used by permission.

about 95% of all such intervals would include the unknown true difference and 5% would not. Suppose, however, that given the side effects and other costs of the new program, the smallest practical and thus acceptable difference (determined during the standard-setting step of the evaluation process) is 15%, then the evaluator will conclude that the 8 percentage-point difference between interventions is not significant from a practical, health perspective although it is statistically significant.

Evaluation 2. Consider another evaluation with 15 of 25 patients (60%) responding to a new program in cancer-pain management and 13 of 25 (52%) responding to a traditional program. The sample size is $\frac{1}{32}$ of that in the first example. The *P* value is 0.57 in this evaluation, in contrast to *P* = 0.001 in the larger evaluation. These *P*s correspond to the same observed 8-percentage-point difference. In this evaluation, the 95% CI extends from −19% to 35%; these values are statistically indistinguishable from the observed difference of 8 percentage points. The larger evaluation permits a more precise estimate of the true value. The greater width of the interval also shows the greater uncertainty that is produced in an estimate based on a smaller sample. Thus the use of a confidence interval enables the evaluator to assess statistical and practical significance.

GUIDELINES FOR ESTABLISHING PRACTICAL SIGNIFICANCE

A difference in outcome between two groups in a program evaluation is significant in a practical sense when its 95% confidence interval is completely above the smallest practical or clinically important difference (see Figure 7.4, page 147).

As can be seen from the chart, the confidence interval (3% to 13%) obtained for Evaluation 1 falls below the desired 15-point difference; it is not practically significant. The difference between groups obtained in Evaluation 2 (−19% to 35%) contains the smallest difference, so no definite conclusion about practical and clinical significance is possible.

Evaluation 3. In this evaluation, 15 of 25 (60%) and 9 of 25 (36%) of patients benefit from the new and traditional programs. The confidence interval for the difference (60% − 36% = 24%) is −3% to 51%. The *P* value (found in a table in a statistics text) is equal to or greater than .05, which is not statistically significant. The confidence interval and *P* are related; if the interval contains 0, then the *P* is not significant. In this case, 0% can be found in the −3% to 51% interval. But 0% is only one of many values inside the confidence interval. The evaluator cannot state: "No meaningful difference"; because much of the interval falls above the 15-point-difference cutoff, the results can be interpreted as practically or clinically inconclusive.

Evaluation 4. In this evaluation, 240 of 400 patients (60%) respond to the new program, while 144 of 400 (36%) respond to the traditional or standard one. The difference is 24% and the 95% CI is 17% to 31%. The difference is statistically ($P < 0.05$) and practically significant.

Eval.	% Responding to Treatment		P Value	Statistical Significance	Difference in % responding		Graph of 95% CI (● = point estimate)	Clinical Significance
	New	Standard			Point Estimate	95% CI		
1	480/800 = 60%	416/800 = 52%	0.001	Yes	8%	3% to 13%		No
2	15/25 = 60%	13/25 = 52%	0.57	No	8%	-19% to 35%		Inconclusive
3	15/25 = 60%	9/25 = 36%	0.09	No	24%	-3% to 51%		Inconclusive
4	240/400 = 60%	144/400 = 36%	<0.0001	Yes	24%	17% to 31%		Yes

-20% -10% 0% 10% 20% 30% 40% 50%

Zero Difference   Smallest Clinically Important Difference Assumed to be 15%

Figure 7.4. Statistical Significance and Clinical Significance Using 95% Confidence Intervals (CI) of Differences Between Patients in Two Programs

SOURCE: Braitman, L. E. (1991). Confidence intervals assess both clinical and statistical significance. *Annals of Internal Medicine*, 114, 515-517. Reproduced with permission.

Proceed With Caution:
Screening and Transforming Data

Before analyzing the data, the entire data set should be reviewed. A first step is to screen for outliers and incorrect values. Outliers are observations that are not consistent with the rest of the data set. For example, an outlier might consist of just 1 of 15 clinics with uncharacteristically very low patient satisfaction scores. Including the clinic's data might bias the results; but excluding it might also do the same, and, in addition, the exclusion might be unethical. The evaluator who finds outliers in the data set could run the main analysis twice: with and without the outlier. In this way, the effects of the outlier can be determined and the results used in deciding how to handle the outlier.

An evaluation's data should also be screened for incorrect values, that is, erroneous statistics. For example, if an evaluation of a program to improve the health care of elderly veterans finds data on veterans who are 2 or 22 years of age, the ages may be errors in data entry.

Another issue that should be resolved before analysis is what do about missing values. **Missing values** refers to data that are not collected from an individual or other sampling unit. Suppose an evaluator needed information on nurses' attitudes toward their working conditions. Suppose also that, of 100 nurses, only 75 respond to all questions on an attitude survey. If a complete set of information on all nurses is necessary for the analysis, then the evaluation's sample size must be treated as 75 and not as 100 respondents. Another example of missing values is failure on the part of all or nearly all people to provide data on a variable. This can happen, for example, if nearly all nurses fail to respond to one or more items on the survey of their attitudes. In this situation, the evaluator should probably exclude the items from the analysis.

Data may also need to be transformed or changed from one scale to another. Linear transformations are made for convenience and involve a change in the mean and a scaling factor. This occurs, for example, when the z transformation is used, and the mean of a distribution is expressed as 0 and its standard deviation (a measure of dispersion) is 1. Nonlinear transformations result in changing the shape of the distribution so that they become normal; statistical tests, like the t-test, can then be used. With rank transformations, observations are rank ordered from lowest to highest. The rank transformation is appropriate when observations are skewed.

The Codebook

The main purpose of preparing a codebook is to make a data set comprehensible to anyone who would like to use it. The codebook can be begun as soon as the analysis plan is agreed upon (say, after you are sure of the evaluation questions and measures), but it should be made final after the completion of data screening and cleaning. Usually, the codebook contains a number for each variable, its location (the column in which it can be found), a name for the variable (of eight or fewer characters in capital letters to accommodate common statistical packages), and a brief description of the meaning of each code. Figure 7.5 is a portion of a codebook for a data set collected from a survey of the postpartum status of women who had partici- pated in one of three projects constituting a prenatal care program.

Variable Number	Variable Location (Column)	Variable Name	Description and Comments
1	1-5	PROJID	A five-digit ID project code; use 99999 for missing values.
2	6-9	INDIVID	A four-digit ID individual code; use 9999 for missing values.
3	10-15	DLIVDATE	Enter mo/day/yr using 2 digits for each segment. May 20, 1992 = 052092. Use 99 for any missing segment; use 999999 if entire date is missing.
4	16-21	FOLLDATE	Use same procedure as for DLIVDATE.
5	22	POSPARVIS	No = 1, Yes = 2, Don't know = 3, use 9 for missing.
6	23-28	VISTDATE	Follow DLIVDATE procedure. If POST-PARTUM VISIT = NO, use 888888. Use 999999 if missing.
7	36-37	WELVISIT	Use 2 digits: 1 = 01, 2 = 02, and so on. Use 00 if none, and 99 if missing.

Figure 7.5. Portions of a Codebook

Meta-Analysis:
A Superanalysis of Evaluation Data

Meta-analysis is a method for combining studies that address the same research questions. The idea is that the larger numbers obtained from contrib- uting studies have greater statistical power and generalizability together than any of the individual studies. Meta-analyses provide a quantitative alternative to the traditional review article in which experts use judgment and intuition to reach conclusions about the merits of a treatment or program or, alterna- tively, base their conclusions on a count of the number of positive versus negative and inconclusive studies.

Suppose a meta-analysis were conducted to answer the question, "Do programs to educate adolescents result in improved decisions about health care?" (See Figure 7.6.) The evaluator answers the question by completing the tasks on p. 150.

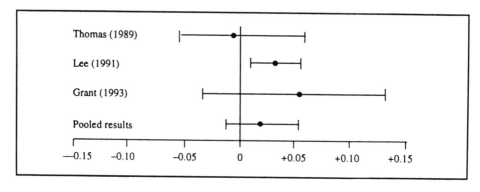

Figure 7.6. Meta-Analysis of 3 Educational Programs for Adolescent Health Care

---

Tasks to Complete in Conducting a Meta-Analysis

1. State the problem, in this case, whether programs to educate adolescents improve their decisions about their own health care.
2. Identify all studies that address the problem.
3. Prepare a scale to rate the quality of the studies.
4. Have at least two people review and rate the quality.
5. Include all studies that meet the criteria for quality, according to the reviewer's ratings of quality.
6. Calculate the difference in improvement between adolescents who were educated and those who were not and plot the difference as a point on a chart.
7. Calculate the chances that the study can be repeated and produce the same results; the statistical range will be shown as a line on the chart.

The three hypothetical evaluations (illustrated in Figure 7.6) show that the weight of the results suggests that programs to educate adolescents have no advantage over the controls.

Although meta-analysis has its origins in psychology and education, it has become associated with epidemiology and medicine. Meta-analyses have been used to summarize a number of diverse investigations, including care of pregnant women, the effects of estrogen replacement therapy on breast cancer, the influence of oat bran on lipid levels, and the treatment of heart attack.

The methods of meta-analysis are continually advancing. Techniques for cumulative meta-analyses, for example, permit the identification of the year when the combined results of multiple studies first achieved a given level of statistical significance. The technique also reveals whether the temporal trend seems to be toward superiority of one program or intervention or another, and it allows assessment of the impact of each new study on the pooled estimate of the treatment effect.

Meta-analyses have not been used to combine the results of program evaluations because too few scientifically appropriate studies have been conducted on any single topic to make the effort worthwhile. Nevertheless, familiarity with the tasks included in a meta-analysis is important because of the evaluator's need to perform many, if not all, of them and to review and use the results. All meta-analyses require a review of the literature to identify eligible studies, the preparation and use of a measure of the quality of the literature, a review of the literature to select studies for the meta-analysis, and the analysis and interpretation of the results. At the minimum, evaluators must be able to review the literature in a systematic fashion because data from published and unpublished sources are used to help set standards of program performance; determine sample size; provide paradigms of research design, measurement, data analysis, and presentation; explain the context in which the current evaluation is conducted; and demonstrate how the current evaluation's findings will add to current knowledge.

SUMMARY AND TRANSITION TO THE NEXT CHAPTER ON EVALUATION REPORTS

This chapter discussed the types of analysis that are particularly useful in program evaluations. Before choosing a method of analysis, the evaluator should determine the number of variables and the characteristics of the data describing or measuring each: nominal, ordinal, or numerical. When using tests of significance, the evaluator should decide on practical as well as statistical meaning.

The next chapter discusses written and oral reports. It addresses the contents of written reports, including objectives, methods, results, conclusions, discussion, and recommendations. Special emphasis is placed on the use of tables and figures to present data. The chapter also explains the contents of an abstract. Because much of evaluation reporting is oral, the chapter provides guidelines for the preparation of visual aids such as overhead transparencies and slides.

EXERCISE: ANALYIZING EVALUATION DATA

Directions

1. For each of the following situations, describe the independent and dependent variables and determine whether they will be described with nominal, ordinal, or numerical data.

Situation	Describe independent and dependent variable.	Tell if the data are nominal, ordinal, or numerical (interval/ratio)
Patients in the experimental and control group tell whether painkillers give complete, moderate, or very little relief.		
Participants in the program are grouped according to whether they are severely, moderately, or marginally depressed and are given a survey of anxiety that is scored from 1 to 9.		
Children are chosen for the evaluation according to whether they have had all recommended vaccinations or not; they are followed for 5 years and their health status is monitored.		
Men and women with stage 1, 2, and 3 of a disease are compared in the quality of life as measured by scores ranging from 1 to 50 that are obtained from standardized observations.		
RNs and LVNs are surveyed, and their average scores are compared.		

2. Use the following information to select and justify a method of data analysis.

Evaluation question: After program participation, is domestic violence decreased?

Standard: A statistically significant difference in domestic violence is found in families who have participated in the experimental program as compared with the control program.

Independent variable: Group membership (experimental versus control)

Design: An experimental design with concurrent controls

Sampling: Eligible participants are assigned at random to an experimental and a control group; 100 participants are in each group (a statistically derived sample size).

Dependent variable: Domestic violence

Types of data: Data on domestic violence will come from the DONT Survey, a 50-point measure in which lower scores mean less violence.

3. Suppose the evaluation of the program to reduce domestic violence is concerned with finding out how younger and older persons compare in the experimental and control groups. Assuming the use of the DONT Survey, which produces numerical scores, which statistical method would be appropriate? Explain.

Suggested Readings

Afifi, A. A., & Clark, V. (1990). *Computer-aided multivariate analysis.* New York: Van Nostrand Reinhold.

> A textbook on multivariate analysis with a practical approach. Discusses data entry, data screening, data reduction, and data analysis. Also explains the options available in different statistical packages.

Antman, E. M., Lau, J., Kupelnick, B., Mosteller, F., & Chalmers, T. C. (1992). A comparison of the results of meta-analyses of randomized controlled trials and recommendations of clinical experts. *Journal of the American Medical Association, 268,* 240-248.

> Provides details on how to conduct a literature review and a meta-analysis, and it has an excellent set of references.

Braitman, L. (1991). Confidence intervals assess both clinical and statistical significance. *Annals of Internal Medicine, 114,* 515-517.

> This brief article contains one of the clearest explanations anywhere of the use of confidence intervals and is highly recommended.

Dawson-Saunders, B., & Trapp, R. G. (1990). *Basic and clinical biostatistics.* East Norwalk, CT: Appleton & Lange.

> A basic and essential primer on the use of statistics in medicine and medical care settings. Explains study designs and how to summarize and present data; it also discusses sampling and the main statistical methods used in analyzing data.

Lau, J., Antman, E. M., Jimenez-Silva, J., Kupelnick, B., Mosteller, F., & Chalmers, T. C. (1992). Cumulative meta-analysis of therapeutic trials for myocardial infarction. *New England Journal of Medicine, 327,* 248-254.

> Describes and demonstrates the technique of cumulative meta-analysis.

Sacks, H. S., Berrier, J., Reitman, D., Anconca-Berk, V. A., & Chalmers, T. C. (1987). Meta-analyses of randomized, controlled trials. *New England Journal of Medicine, 316,* 450-455.

> This is a basic, but technical, explanation of the principles of issues related to meta-analyses in medicine.

Steinberg, K. K., Thacker, S. B., Smith, J., et al. (1991). A meta-analysis of the effect of estrogen replacement therapy on the risk of breast cancer. *Journal of the American Medical Association, 265,* 1985-1990.

> Excellent examples of how to conduct literature reviews, rate studies according to their quality, and conduct a meta-analysis.

Review Notes

Purpose of This Chapter

This chapter focuses on the evaluation report. A report of a completed evaluation answers the evaluation questions, describes how the answers were obtained, and translates the findings into conclusions and recommendations regarding program evaluation, health care, and health policy.

Evaluation reports can be written and oral. The chapter first discusses how to prepare a written report of an evaluation and provides a checklist and scoring sheet for assessing its quality. Figures and tables are used to present evaluation results, and these also are discussed.

The oral presentation is examined next. The emphasis is on preparing visuals (such as overhead transparencies and slides) for 10-minute to 1-hour talks.

8 Evaluation Reports

The Written Evaluation Report

A written report is required of nearly all evaluations. A useful report provides enough information so that at least two interested individuals can agree on the evaluation's purposes, methods, and conclusions. If the report is being submitted to a funding agency, such as a health foundation or the government, the composition and format of the report may be set for you. In most cases, however, evaluators are on their own in deciding on the length and content of the report.

LENGTH

The text of an evaluation report should be between 5,000 and 15,000 words or 20 to 60 double-spaced pages (with standard 10- or 12-pitch type with 12-pitch spacing and 1-inch margins). A list of bibliographic references should accompany the report. Up to 10 tables and 10 figures (such as photographs or graphs) should be adequate. In addition, an abstract of 250 words and a summary of up to 15 pages are often helpful. In the appendix to the report, the evaluator can put working documents such as resumes, project worksheets, survey response frequencies, complex mathematical calculations, copies of measures such as questionnaire surveys or medical record review forms, organizational charts, memorandums, training materials, and project planning documents. Including the appendix, the evaluation report can be more than 100 pages.

Consider the following table of contents for a report of an 18-month program combining diet and exercise to improve health status and quality of life for persons 75 years of age or older (Example 8.1, below). An experimental group of elderly people who still live at home received the program, while another living-at-home group did not. Participants were randomly assigned to the experimental or control groups according to the street on which they live. That is, participants living on Street A were randomly assigned, as were participants living on Streets B, C, and so on. Participants in the evaluation who needed medical services chose freely between two clinics offering differing models of care, one staffed primarily by physicians and the other staffed primarily by nurses. The evaluators investigated whether program participation made a difference in the health and quality of life of men and women and the role of patient mix in making those differences. They also analyzed the cost-effectiveness of the two models of health care delivery.

Example 8.1: Sample Table of Contents for a Report: An Evaluation of the Living-at-Home Program for Elders

Abstract: 250 words
Summary: 8 pages
Text of Report: 41 pages

  I. Introduction: The Health Problem, the Program, and the Evaluation Questions (6 pages)
 II. Methods (10 pages)

Example 8.1 (Continued)

    A. Evaluation Design
    B. Objectives and Activities of the Intervention and Control Programs
    C. Sample
       1. Inclusion and exclusion criteria
       2. Justification of sample sizes
       3. How sample was selected and assigned to groups
    D. Outcome Measures
       1. Reliability and validity of measures of quality of life, health, and cost-effectiveness
       2. Quality assurance system for the data collection
    E. Analysis
       Citing and justifying the specific method used to test each hypothesis or answer each evaluation question. For example, "to compare men and women in their health, we used a *t*-test, and to predict who benefited most from participation in the experimental program, we relied on stepwise multiple regression."

III. Results (15 pages)

    A. Response rates (such as how many eligible men and women agreed to participate in the evaluation; how many completed the entire program; how many individuals completed all data collection requirements)
    B. Demographic and other descriptive characteristics (for the experimental and control groups: number and percentage of men and women; number and percentage under 65 to 75 years of age, 76 to 85, and 85 and older; number and percentage of men and women; and numbers and percentages choosing each of the two health care staffing models)
    C. Effectiveness: Quality of Life and Health Status
    D. Cost-Effectiveness of Two Staffing Models of Care

IV. Conclusions (8 pages)

 V. Recommendations (2 pages)

VI. Tables and Figure

    A. Table 1. Demographic Characteristics of Participants
    B. Table 2. Health Outcomes and Quality of Life for Men and Women with Varying Levels of Illness
    C. Table 3. Costs of Three Clinic Staffing Models
    D. Figure 1. Flowchart: How Participants Were Assigned to Groups by "Cluster"

VII. Appendixes

    A. Copies of all measures
    B. Calculations linking costs and effectiveness
    C. Final sample-size calculations
    D. Testimony from program participants regarding their satisfaction with participation in the experimental program
    E. Informed consent statements
    F. List of panel participants and affiliations
    G. Training materials for all data collection
    H. Data collection quality assurance plan

Written Evaluation Reports:
What Should They Include?

INTRODUCTION

The introduction to an evaluation report has three components: (a) a description of the health problem, (b) an explanation of the means by which the experimental program is to solve the health problem, and (c) a list of questions that the evaluation answers about the merits of the program's solution to the problem. Example 8.2 illustrates the contents of the introduction to a written report.

Example 8.2: What to Include in the Introduction to a Written Report

1. The health problem. Describe the problem that the program and its evaluation are designed to solve. In the description, tell how many people are affected by the problem, and what its human and financial costs are. Cite the literature to defend the estimates of the importance and costs of the problem.

2. The program. Give an overview of the program's objectives and activities and any unique features (such as its size, location, or number and types of participants). If the program has been modeled on some other intervention, describe the similarities and differences and cite references.

3. The evaluation. Give the objectives of the evaluation and state the questions and standards. Establish the connections between the general health problem, the objectives of the program, and the evaluation. That is, tell how the evaluation will provide knowledge about this particular program and also provide new

knowledge about the health problem as in the following example.

Sample Introduction

The purpose of this experimental evaluation is to identify whether community-dwelling elderly who participated in a home health care program improved in their health and quality of life. Participants were randomly assigned to an experimental or a control group. Because evidence exists that home health care can improve social, emotional, and physical functioning in the elderly [references regarding the potential of home health care should have been cited in the first part of the introduction], we asked about the effectiveness of the program for men and women of differing ages and levels of medical and social problems and the nature, characteristics, and costs of effective home health services. We based standards of effectiveness on the comparative performance of the experimental and control groups. . . .

METHODS

The methods section of the report should describe the program, define terms, and describe the design, sample, measures, and analysis.

The program. Describe the experimental and comparison programs. Carefully distinguish between them. How long did each participate in the evaluation? If protocols were prepared to standardize the implementation of the programs, describe them and any training in the use of the protocols that took place.

Definitions. Define all potentially misleading terms such as "quality of life," "health status," "high risk," "accessible care," "high quality of care," and "efficiency." When appropriate, distinguish between practical and statistical significance for the main outcome measures.

Design. Tell whether the evaluation uses an experimental or observational design. If the design was experimental, give the type (e.g., "concurrent controls," in which participants are randomly assigned to experimental and control groups). Specify whether participants were "blinded," that is, did not know if they were in the experimental or control group.

Sample. Give the inclusion and exclusion criteria for participation in the evaluation. Tell whether the participants are randomly selected and randomly assigned. Explain how the sample sizes were determined.

Measures. Describe the characteristics of each measure of the main evaluation questions. Who administered the measure? Was training required? Is the measure reliable? Valid? How much time is required to complete the measure? How many questions does it contain? How were they selected? If appropriate, cite the theory behind the choice of questions or the other measures on which they were based. How is the measure scored?

Analysis. Check each evaluation question for the main variables. Then, for the main variables, describe and justify the analytic method. Are any unusual methods used in the analysis? If there are, these should be described. Name the statistical package in case other evaluators want to perform a similar analysis using the same setup. If a relatively new or complex data-analytic method is used, provide a reference for it.

RESULTS

Present the results of the statistical analyses. Give all response rates and describe the evaluation participants' characteristics. When appropriate, compare the sample who agreed to participate with those who refused or did not complete the entire program or provide complete data. Give the results for each major evaluation question and its subquestions. For example, if a main question asks whether patients' quality of life improves, present the results for that question; when helpful, also provide data on types of individuals (e.g., older men, sicker patients) for whom the program was most and least effective in terms of quality of life.

Use tables and graphs to summarize the results. Example 8.3 contains a table that is typical of one of the first to appear in most reports.

Example 8.3: A Table to Describe the Characteristics of an Evaluation's Participants

Characteristic	Experimental n (%)		Control n (%)		Difference	Confidence Interval
Age (years)						
65-75						
76-85						
86 or more						
Health						
Excellent						
Good						
Fair						
Poor						
Choice of Clinic						
Primarily nurse-run						
Primarily physician-run						

Do *not* interpret data in this section. Statements such as this one: "These results contradict the findings of previous evaluations . . ." belong in the discussion. The following are recommendations for the use of figures and tables.

RECOMMENDATIONS FOR COMPOSING FIGURES AND TABLES IN EVALUATION REPORTS

Using Figures

Figure 8.1 on page 163 is one used to report the results of a study concerned with describing variability in transfusion practice during coronary bypass surgery.

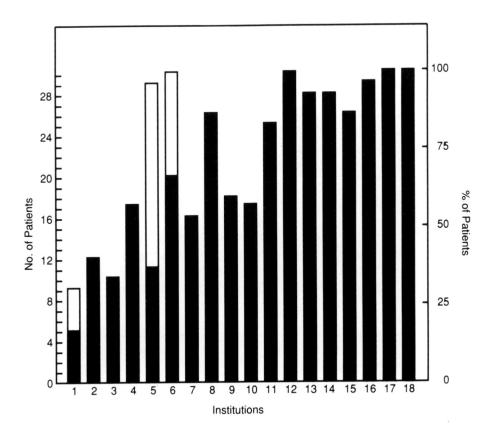

Figure 8.1. Variability in Transfusion Practice During Coronary Artery Bypsss Surgery

SOURCE: Goodnough, L. T., Johnston, M. F. M., Toy, P. T. C. Y., and the Transfusion Medicine Academic Award Group (1991). The variability of transfusion practice in coronary artery bypass graft surgery. *Journal of the American Medical Association. 265,* 286-290. Copyright 1981, 1991, 1992, American Medical Association, reprinted by permission.

NOTE: Number (percentage) of patients transfused with red blood cells among 30 first-time coronary artery bypass graft patients at each institution. The distribution of institutions is expressed as a histogram, indicating the number of institutions each transfusing zero to 30 patients. The distribution of patients who received red blood cells was variable among institutions. Open bars indicate autologous blood; and shaded bars, homologous blood.

Based on the data presented in the figure, the study reported that the variation in the percentage of patients receiving red blood cells among institutions differed significantly (range, 17% to 100%; $P < .001$). Among the study's conclusions was that, in view of the NIH's Consensus Conference programs that addressed perisurgical blood component use, conference recommendations need to be more effectively applied at the institutional level.

The figure conforms to these rules:

1. Place variables (in this case, institutions) that are being compared along the X axis.

2. Place numbers along the Y axis; when appropriate, include percentages on the figure.

3. Make sure that visual differences correspond to meaningful differences. In this case, the authors express the distribution of institutions as a histogram. In a histogram, the area of each bar is proportional to the percentage of observations in that interval (e.g., if 11 of 100 patients were found in an interval labeled 20 to 50 years of age, then the 11 patients would constitute $11/100$ or 11% of the area of the histogram).

4. Include an explanation of the findings (e.g., "The distribution of patients who received red blood cells was variable among institutions.").

5. Include a legend or key (e.g., "Open bars indicate autologous blood; shaded bars, homologous blood.").

Using Tables

1. Put the most important values to be compared in columns. If you are describing the characteristics (such as age or educational level) of users and nonusers of smokeless tobacco (Figure 8.1), the values (such as numbers and percentages of persons with the differing characteristics) go in the columns.

Characteristics	Users N (%)	Nonusers N (%)
Age (years)		
Under 18		
18-25		
26-35		
36-45		
46 and over		
Sex		
Male		
Female		
Years using		
Less than 1		
1-3		
4-6		
more than 6		

Figure 8.2. The Columns: Users and Nonusers of Smokeless Tobacco

2. If appropriate and possible, put statistical values in ascending (largest values) to descending order. Suppose that Figure 8.2 describes the results of

a nationwide survey of 734 people who were asked whether or not they preferred fish or meat for dinner as follows:

	Number of People Choosing:		Total
	Meat	Fish	
Northeast	140	124	264
South	100	52*	152
West	89	138**	227
North Central	45	46	91
Total	374	360	734

Figure 8.3. Statistical Values in Order: The National Dietary Preferences Survey (hypothetical)

NOTE: Survey administered by the Center for Nutrition and Health, Washington, DC
 *$P = .003$
 **$P = .002$

Note that, in this table, the preferences for meat are in descending order. The choice of which values to place first depends upon the points being emphasized. If the evaluation's focus were on preferences for fish, then the first cell of the table under region would have been West.

3. Use a standardized method for calling the reader's attention to key aspects of the table such as statistical significance. For example, *, †, ‡, §, and ¶ are one typical hierarchy.

Figure 8.4 shows the format used to compare the effectiveness of an extensive ethics education intervention, a limited intervention, and a control. It uses a standard hierarchy of symbols.

	Controls		Limited Intervention		Extensive Intervention	
	Before	After	Before	After	Before	After
No.	18	22	4	25	16	9
% Appropriate	78	77	50	52	75†	100‡

Figure 8.4. Percentage of Charts Documenting Appropriate Consent Conversation: Effects of Education*

NOTES: *"Appropriate" is defined as speaking to patient if patient is competent, or to surrogate if patient is incompetent.
 † Not significantly different from Controls + Limited before the intervention.
 ‡ Significantly greater than Controls + Limited after the intervention ($P < .95$).

SOURCE: Sulmasy, D. P., Geller, G., Faden, R., and Levine, D. M. (1992). The quality of mercy: Caring for patients with "Do not resuscitate orders." *Journal of the American Medical Association, 267*, 682-686. Copyright 1981, 1991, 1992, American Medical Association; reprinted by permission.

The investigators report that the rate of documentation of an appropriate consent conversation with the patient or surrogate, while not significantly different among the groups at baseline, rose from 75% to 100% in the extensive intervention group. Moreover, the investigators report that the postintervention rate was significantly higher for the extensive intervention group than for the controls and the limited intervention groups ($P < .05$).

CONCLUSIONS OR DISCUSSION

Tell what the results mean by answering questions such as the following:

♦ Taking the broadest perspective, what can you conclude from the evaluation? Is the program any good? For whom? Under what circumstances? An illustration of one answer to these questions comes from the first sentences in the "Comments" section of a report of an evaluation of an ethics education intervention for physicians in Example 8.4:

Example 8.4: Conclusions of an Evaluation of an Ethics Education Intervention

"This study has examined the quality of care for patients with DNR [Do Not Resuscitate] orders as it is reflected in the documentation of attention to such important considerations as informed consent and the appropriateness of a variety of other CCCs [concurrent care concerns, e.g., intubation, dialysis, blood product support] that are not specified by the DNR order itself. We conclude that the quality of such care can be improved by an extensive ethics education intervention for medical house officers and that quality varies systematically according to the patient's diagnosis."

SOURCE: D. P. Sulmasy, G. Geller, R. Faden, and D. M. Levine. (1992). The quality of mercy: Caring for patients with "Do not resuscitate orders." *Journal of the American Medical Association, 267,* 682-686. Copyright 1981, 1991, 1992, American Medical Association; reprinted by permission.

In addition, the evaluation report should consider answering the following questions:

♦ Did the program achieve its goals and objectives?
♦ For which participants was the program most effective?
♦ For which participants was the program least effective?
♦ Which components of the program were most/least effective?
♦ How do the results of this evaluation compare in whole or in part with the findings of other studies?
♦ What new knowledge about the health, health program evaluation, policy, and the system can be learned from this evaluation?

- What gaps in knowledge have been revealed by this evaluation?
- What are the limitations (due to imperfections in the design, sample, measurement, and analysis), and how do these affect the conclusions?

RECOMMENDATIONS

When making recommendations, consider answering questions such as these:

1. Without changing its basic goals and objectives, if the program were to be redone to remove its flaws, what are the top five changes or additions that should be considered?
2. If the program were to be applied to another setting or group of participants, who is likely to benefit most?
3. If the program were to be instituted in the same or some other setting, what are the costs to expect?
4. What objectives should be changed or added to the program to expand its scope and effectiveness?

THE ABSTRACT

The abstract of an evaluation report is usually between 200 and 300 words. Its purpose is to present the evaluation's main objectives, methods, and findings. The following topics must be considered when writing the abstract, although the amount of detail will vary.

Objective: In one or two sentences, tell the purpose of the evaluation.

Design: Using a standard term, name the design. Use terms such as "randomized controlled" (true experiment) or "nonrandomized" (quasi experiment), or "survey." Describe any unique feature of the design such as the use of blinding.

Participants: Describe the characteristics of the participants including the number of participants in the experimental and control groups; demographics (such as age, income, and health status); region of the country; and size of facility (such as hospital, clinic, school). Describe any unique features of the participants such as their location or special health characteristics.

Main outcome measures: For each dependent variable in the evaluation question, describe the surveys, records reviews, tests, and observations that were used. Describe any unique features of the measures and include any special notes on reliability or validity.

Results: For each major dependent variable, give the results.

Conclusions: In one or two sentences, explain what the results mean. Did the program work? Is it applicable to other participants?

An illustration of an annotated abstract is given in Figure 8.5. It comes from an evaluation of the impact of ethics education on the knowledge, confidence, and practices of house officers regarding ethical issues.

Objective. — To assess (1) the effect of an ethics education intervention for medical house officers on practices surrounding "Do Not Resuscitate" (DNR) orders and (2) the association of DNR care with patient diagnosis and demographic variables.

Design. — A 1-year randomized, controlled trial.

Setting. — An urban, university teaching hospital.

Participants. — Eighty-eight internal medicine house officers.

Intervention. — House officers were arbitrarily assigned to four "firms." One firm was randomized to an extensive ethics education intervention (EI), one to a limited intervention, and two served as controls.

Main Outcome Measures. — Charts of patients with DNR orders were reviewed for compliance with the hospital's DNR policy, which instructs that when DNR orders are written there should be (1) an attending signature, (2) document of reasons, (3) appropriate consent, and (4) attention to 11 concurrent care concerns (CCCs) (e.g., the appropriateness of intubation, tube feedings, hospice).

Results. — Thirty-nine charts were reviewed before the intervention and 57 after. The number of CCCs per DNR order fell among patients cared for by controls (1.9 to 1.0, $P < .05$) and rose among patients cared for by the EI group (0.9 to 3.8, $P < .05$). Compliance with the DNR policy varied among patients with differing diagnoses. "Do Not Resuscitate" orders were signed less frequently ($P = .01$) for patients with the acquired immunodeficiency syndrome (AIDS) (65%) compared with patients who had other diagnoses (85%) or malignancy (91%). Similarly, appropriate consent was recorded for 59% of patients with AIDS, 83% of others, and 85% of those with malignancy ($P < .05$). The number of CCCs per DNR was 0.7 for AIDS, 1.4 for others, and 2.4 for malignancy ($P < .05$). In multivariate regression analysis, house officer ethics education and patient diagnosis, but not patient gender, age, race, or insurance status, were predictors of the number of CCCs per DNR.

Conclusions. — (1) An extensive ethics education intervention can improve care for DNR patients, especially with respect to CCCs. (2) In this setting, quality of care for DNR patients varied systematically with diagnosis. These results have implications for the design and implementation of ethics education programs.

Figure 8.5. Illustrative Annotated Abstract

SOURCE: D. P. Sulmasy, G. Geller, R. Faden, and D. M. Levine. (1992). The quality of mercy: Caring for patients with "Do Not Resuscitate orders." *Journal of the American Medical Association, 267,* 682-686. Copyright 1981, 1991, 1992, American Medical Association; reprinted by permission.

THE EXECUTIVE SUMMARY

An executive summary provides all potential users with an easy-to-read report of the evaluation's major purposes, methods, findings, and recommendations. The summary usually varies in length from 3 to 15 pages. Executive summaries are nearly always required by evaluation funders who frequently specify the number of pages that are expected.

Three rules must govern the preparation of the summary:

1. Include the important purposes, methods, findings, and recommendations
2. Avoid jargon

   Poor:
   We used a *cluster sampling strategy* in which hospitals were assigned at random . . .

   Better:
   We assigned hospitals at random . . .

   Poor:
   We established *concurrent validity by correlating scores* on Measure A with those on Measure B.

   Better:
   We examined the relationship between scores on Measures A and B.

3. Use active verbs

   Poor:
   The use of health care services *was found* by the evaluation to be more frequent in people under 45 years of age.

   Better:
   The evaluation found more frequent use of services by people under 45 years of age.

   Poor:
   It is recommended that the prevention of prematurity be the focus of prenatal care education.

   Better:
   We recommend that the prevention of prematurity by the focus of prenatal care education.

The following topics should guide the preparation of the executive summary:

The Program or Intervention. Describe the intervention or program's purposes and objectives, settings, and unique features. Consider answering questions like these:

1. During which years did the intervention take place?
2. Who were the funders?
3. How did the intervention differ from others that have similar purposes?
4. How great was the need for the intervention?

The Evaluation. Give an overview of the purposes of the evaluation, describe the evaluation questions and standards, review the design and sample, discuss the outcomes and how they were measured, and explain the main analytic methods. Consider answering questions like these:

1. How was evaluation defined?
2. Are the evaluation methods unique in any way?
3. For whom are the evaluation's findings and recommendations most applicable?
4. Who performed the evaluation?
5. During which years did the evaluation take place?

The Findings. Give the answers to the evaluation questions. Tell if the program or intervention was effective. Did it achieve agreed-upon standards of merit? Consider answering questions like these:

1. Is the intervention likely to be sustained over time?
2. Who benefited most (and least) from participation?

Conclusions. Tell whether the intervention solved the problem it was designed to solve. Were the findings consistent with those of evaluations of similar interventions? What is the bottom line? Did the intervention succeed? If so, explain the reasons for success. If the intervention did not succeed, explain the reasons for failure.

Recommendations. Tell other evaluators, researchers, and policy-makers about the implications of the evaluation. Explain the changes to the program or intervention that could make it more effective. Describe the participants who are most likely to be in need of the intervention in the future. Describe ways to improve future interventions and evaluations.

Reviewing Your Report

After completing an evaluation report, it should be reviewed to determine the extent to which it conforms to acceptable standards. The following "scoring" sheet (Figure 8.6) is provided as a guide. It can also be used to review a variety of evaluation manuscripts and reports.

Scale: 4 = definitely yes
        3 = probably yes
        2 = probably no
        1 = definitely no
        0 = no data; uncertain
        NA = not applicable

CRITERIA: PRECISION OF OBJECTIVES JUSTIFICATION OF STANDARDS	RATING SCALE					
	4	3	2	1	0	NA
Are the evaluation's objectives/questions/hypotheses stated precisely?						
Are the standards clear?						
Are practical standards justified?						
Are statistical standards justified?						
Other?						

CRITERIA: NEED FOR THE EVALUATION	RATING SCALE					
	4	3	2	1	0	NA
Is the need for the evaluation justified?						
Is the current evaluation placed within the context of previous work?						
Are criteria given for any literature that is reviewed?						
Is the quality of the reviewed literature assessed?						
Does the current evaluation continue the work of others?						
Does the current evaluation build on the previous work of others?						
Does the current evaluation fill in gaps in knowledge?						
Other?						

Figure 8.6. Reviewing Evaluations: A Scoring Guide

NOTE: Scale: 4 = definitely yes; 3 = probably yes; 2 = probably no; 1 = definitely no; 0 = no data, uncertain; NA = not applicable.

CRITERIA: DESCRIPTION OF THE INTERVENTION	RATING SCALE					
	4	3	2	1	0	NA
Is the importance of the health problem to be solved by the program justified?						
Are experimental program goals and objectives specified?						
Are descriptions given of the special features of the experimental program?						
Are quality assurance systems in place for monitoring the implementation of the experimental program?						
Is the experimental program standardized within sites?						
Is the experimental progran. dardized across sites?						
Are the resources of the experimental program described?						
Are the settings in which the experimental program takes place described?						
Are control group program goals and objectives specified?						
Are descriptions given of the implementation of the control group program?						
Are quality assurance systems in place for monitoring the implementation of the control group program?						
Is the control group program standardized within sites?						
Is the control group program standardized across sites?						
Are the resources of the control program described?						
Are the settings in which the control program takes place described?						
Are the effects on the evaluation's generalizability given for failure to have uniform program goals, objectives, protocols, settings, or resources?						
Other?						

Figure 8.6. (Continued)

CRITERIA: EVALUATION DESIGN AND SAMPLING	RATING SCALE					
	4	3	2	1	0	NA
Is the entire population included?						
If a sample, are sampling methods adequately described?						
If a sample, are the evaluation's participants randomly selected?						
If more than one group, are the evaluation's participants randomly assigned?						
If the unit that is sampled (e.g., patients) is not the population of main concern (e.g., physicians), is this properly addressed in the analysis or discussion?						
If a sample and a nonrandom sampling method are used is evidence given regarding the similarity of the groups at baseline?						
If groups are not equivalent at baseline, is this problem adequately addressed in analysis or interpretation?						
Are criteria given for including all evaluation units (e.g., patients, physicians, and whoever else is studied)?						
Are criteria given for excluding evaluation units?						
Is the sample size justified (say, with a power calculation)?						
Is information given on the number of participants in the source population?						
Is information given on the number of participants eligible to participate?						
Is information given on the number who agreed to participate?						
Is information given on the number who refused to participate?						
Is information given on the number who dropped out or were lost to follow-up before completing all elements of data collection?						
Is information given on the number who completed all elements of data collection?						
Is information given on the number for whom some data are missing?						

Figure 8.6. (Continued)

CRITERIA: **EVALUATION DESIGN AND SAMPLING (continued)**	RATING SCALE					
	4	3	2	1		NA
Are participants measured over time?						
If observations or measures are made over time, is the time period justified?						
Are participants blinded?						
Are reasons given for individuals or groups who dropped out?						
Are reasons given for missing data?						
Are the effects on generalizability of choice, equivalence, and participation of the resultant sample explained?						
Are the effects on internal validity of choice, equivalence, and participation of the resultant sample explained?						
Other?						

CRITERIA: **JUSTIFICATION AND VALIDITY OF DATA SOURCES AND DATA COLLECTION**	RATING SCALE					
	4	3	2	1	0	NA
Are the independent variables defined?						
Are the dependent variables defined?						
Are data provided on the reliability of data sources for the main variables?						
Are data provided on the validity of data sources for the main variables?						
Is the reliability of each data source adequate?						
Is the validity of each data source adequate?						
Are the data collection methods adequately described?						
Is information provided on methods for ensuring the quality of data collection?						
Is the length of the data collection period justified?						
Is the length of the data collection period sufficient for the evaluation's objectives?						
Are the effects on the research's generalizability of the selection, reliability, validity of data sources, and the length of data collection explained?						
Other?						

Figure 8.6. (Continued)

CRITERIA: APPROPRIATENESS OF DATA ANALYSIS	RATING SCALE					
	4	3	2	1	0	NA
Are statistical methods adequately described?						
Are statistical methods justified?						
Is the purpose of the analysis clear?						
Are scoring systems described?						
Are potential confounders adequately controlled for in the analysis?						
Are analytic specifications of the independent and dependent variables consistent with the evaluation questions or hypotheses under study?						
Is the unit of analysis specified clearly?						
Is a sensitivity analysis performed to account for imprecise measurements or uncertain outcomes?						
Other?						

CRITERIA: COMPLETENESS AND ACCURACY OF REPORTING	RATING SCALE					
	4	3	2	1	0	NA
Are references given for complex statistical methods?						
Are complex statistical methods described in an appendix?						
Are exact *P* values given?						
Are confidence intervals given?						
Are the results of the analysis clearly described?						
Are the evaluation's results clearly described?						
Do the conclusions follow from the study's results?						
Other?						

Figure 8.6. (Continued)

CRITERIA: BOUNDARIES OF THE EVALUATION	RATING SCALE					
	4	3	2	1	0	NA
Are the evaluation's biases explained?						
Are the results practical?						
Are the uses of the evaluation's findings clear?						
Are directives given for future evaluations?						
Are directives given for policy decisions?						
Are ethical considerations included?						
Other?						

Figure 8.6. (Continued)

Oral Reporting

An oral report of a program evaluation may consist of an account of some or all of its objectives, methods, and findings. All reports can be reinforced by providing listeners with visual aids. The most common of these are slides and overhead transparencies. Slides are more expensive to produce than overheads and take more time to produce. As modes of presentation, slides have the reputation of being more "polished," but the comparative effectiveness of the two has not been evaluated.

The following recommendations can help in the preparation of 10-minute to 1-hour oral presentations in which slides or overheads are used to complement the evaluator's report.

RECOMMENDATIONS FOR THE PREPARATION OF AN ORAL PROGRAM EVALUATION REPORT

1. Do the talking and explaining and let the audience listen. Use visuals to focus the audience's attention on the key points of the talk. Do not require listeners to read and listen at the same time.

Poor:

Reliability

A reliable measure is one that is relatively free from measurement error. Because of this error, individuals' obtained scores are different than their true scores. In some cases, the error results from the measure itself: It may be difficult to understand or poorly administered.

Better:

Reliability

- Reliable measures are relatively free of error.
- Causes of measurement error:
  - Measure is hard to understand.
  - Measure is poorly administered.

    The second visual is better than the first because the listener can more easily keep the main points in view without being diverted by the first visual's reading requirements. If the objective is to have the audience read something, then a handout (with time out for reading) is more appropriate than a visual.

2. Each visual aid should have a title.

3. During the talk, address the talk's purposes and the evaluations's purposes, main methods, main results, conclusions, and recommendations. A typical oral evaluation report covers the following:

   A. *Title of the talk and names and affiliations of the evaluators*

**Children and Prevention (CAP):
What the Evaluation Found**

Prepared by
Jane Austen, Ph.D.
Louis Pasteur, M.D.
Michael Jackson, R.N.

*The Center for Program Evaluation
in the Health Professions*

   B. *What the evaluation is about*

Goal of the Evaluation of CAP

- To appraise impact
- To determine costs
- To estimate benefits

C. The purpose of the report

Purpose

Describe and compare children in CAP with other children in the following areas:

- Knowledge of selected health promotion activities
- Health status

D. A description of the program

The Children and Health (CAP) Program

- Goal is to improve health prevention knowledge and behavior of children
- Begin education as early as 3 years of age
- 3-year community elementary school program
- $3 million
- Sponsored by the Education Trustees, a nonprofit health promotion group

---

E. A description of the participants

Who Was in CAP?

- 500 children between the ages of 4 and 7 years
- Six public schools: three in the experiment and three in the control groups
- Assignment of schools to groups was random
- Control schools have no special health promotion activities

---

F. A description and explanation of the main outcome measures
(The description and explanation can include information on reliability and validity and samples of the content of the measures.)

How Was Information Collected?

- Tests of knowledge
- Interviews with students
- Interviews with parents
- Review of attendance records
- Medical records review

G. An accounting of the main results, as in the following hypothetical table

Knowledge: How the CAPs and the Control Compare

Age	Experimental Scores	Control Scores
4	45	22*
5	46	20*
6	33	29
7	35	32

HIGHER SCORES ARE BETTER
* = STATISTICALLY SIGNIFICANT

Notice that no decimals are used; numbers should be rounded up to the nearest whole number.

H. Conclusions

Conclusion

- Younger children benefit more than older children.

I. Alternative explanations, limitations, problems

Do the Results Fit?

- Few valid evaluations of preventive programs
  and young children
- No outside programs on prevention during period
  of evaluation

  - Checked content of health education
    classes
  - Checked movie and television listings

J. Recommendations

Recommendations

- Adopt CAP for 4- and 5-year-olds.
- Revise the program and evaluate
  again for 6- and 7-year-olds.

---

4. Keep tables and figures simple. Explain the meaning of the title, the column and row headings, and the statistics. For the table on page 181, you can say:

> The next slide compares the knowledge of children in CAP with those in the controls. We used the CAP Test, in which higher scores are better, and the highest score is 50 points.
>
> As you can see [if possible, point to the appropriate place on the screen], children who are 4 and 5 did significantly better in CAP. We found no differences in children who were 6 and 7.

5. Check carefully for typographical errors.

6. Avoid abbreviations and acronyms unless you are certain that the listener has been informed and knows what they mean. In the example of the CAP, its acronym was explained in the first visual. If necessary, explain and define each abbreviation and acronym.

7. Outline or write out the talk.

8. Rehearse the presentation before you create the final copies of the visual aids. Then rehearse again. The purpose of the first rehearsal is to make sure that the talk is logical, that the spelling is correct, and that the arrangement of words, figures, and tables is meaningful.

9. Ensure that visuals are easy to see. Horizontal placement is better than vertical. All potential listeners should be able to see the visuals. In advance of the talk, check the room, the seating plan, and the place where you will stand. If you are using slides, hold them up against the light before use. If you cannot see the contents, the audience will not be able to see them either.

10. Use humor and rhetorical questions to engage listeners. Typical rhetorical questions are given in three of the visuals above: Who was in CAP? How was information collected? Do the results fit?

EXERCISE: EVALUATION REPORTS

Directions

1. Review Visual Aid 1. If necessary, improve it.

VISUAL AID 1

A **stratified random sample** is one in which the population is divided into subgroups or "strata," and a random sample is then selected from each group. For example, in a program to teach women about options for treatment for breast cancer, the evaluator can sample from a number of subgroups including women of differing ages (under 19 years, 20 to 30, 31 to 35, over 35) and income (high, medium, low).

2. Write the text for the following table of data. The data were obtained in an evaluation of audit and feedback and local opinion leader education as methods of encouraging compliance among physicians with a guideline for the management of women patients with a previous cesarean section.

| | % of Eligible Cases by Group* | | | Difference Between Opinion Leader Education Group and Control and Audit and Feedback Groups Combined | | |
	Control	Audit and Feedback	Opinion Leader Education	%	F Test†	P
Offered a trial of labor	51.3 (43.5-59.2)	56.3 (45.2-67.4)	74.2 (63.1-85.2)	+40	10.13	.002
Underwent a trial of labor	28.3 (23.0-33.7)	21.4 (13.9-29.0)	38.2 (30.6-45.7)	+46	7.86	.007
Vaginal birth	14.5 (10.3-18.7)	11.8 (5.8-17.7)	25.3 (19.3-31.2)	+85	9.74	.003
Elective cesarean section	66.8 (61.7-72.0)	69.7 (62.4-77.0)	53.7 (46.5-61.0)	−21	11.37	.001
Unscheduled cesarean section	18.7 (15.4-22.1)	18.6 (13.9-23.2)	21.4 (16.8-26.1)	+14	1.96	.166
Before labor	1.7	3.5	1.7	...	...	...
Latent labor‡	11.7	7.5	11.8	...	...	...
Active labor‡	5.3	7.6	7.9	...	...	...

Table: Delivery Outcomes by Study Group

NOTES: *Numbers in parentheses are 95% confidence limits.
   †For each F test, df = 1.74.
   ‡Latent labor defined as dilatation less than 3 cm; active labor as dilatation of 3 cm or greater.

SOURCE: J. Lomas, M. Enkin, G. M. Anderson, W. J. Hannah, E. Vayda, and J. Singer. (1991). Opinion leaders vs. audit and feedback to implement practice guidelines. *Journal of the American Medical Association, 265,* 2022-2207. Copyright 1981/91/92, American Medical Association; reprinted by permission.

Suggested Readings

Bailar, J. C., & Mosteller, F. (1988). Guidelines for statistical reporting in articles for medical journals. *Annals of Internal Medicine, 108,* 266-273.

> The title of this article suggests that it is primarily appropriate for articles in medical journals. People with other interests, however, can benefit from the discussion on figures and tables and on the merits of confidence intervals and exact *P* values.

Bates, E. S., & Abemayor, E. (1991). Slide presentation graphics using a personal computer. *Archives of Otolaryngology and Head and Neck Surgery, 117,* 1026-1030.

> An evaluation of four graphics programs for making slides. Although out-of-date in terms of technology and cost, the criteria used by the authors are still relevant.

Lin, Yu-Chong. (1989). Practical approaches to scientific presentation. *Chinese Journal of Physiology, 32,* 71-78.

> Describes the purposes, language, and style of oral presentation, with particular emphasis on using slides in scientific presentations.

Pfeiffer, W. S. (1991). *Technical writing.* New York: Macmillan.

> Provides useful tips on the details of putting together formal reports. Discusses the cover and title page, table of contents, and executive summary. It also contains rules for preparing charts and giving oral presentations. Its orientation is for business, but many of the lessons can be adapted to program evaluation.

Spinler, S. (1991). How to prepare and deliver pharmacy presentations. *American Journal of Hospital Pharmacy, 48,* 1730-1738.

> Provides extremely useful tips on the preparation and use of slides. Also discusses how to rehearse and then deliver an oral presentation.

Review Notes

Answers to Exercises

CHAPTER 1

1. What are the evaluation questions?
   - To what extent have key curriculum objectives been achieved?
   - How enduring are the effects? (For example, did quality of care improve?)
   - For which groups was the program most effective? (For example, do differences exist in knowledge between faculty and residents?)

2. What are the standards?

   Although not explicitly stated, they probably are improvements over time.

3. What is the design?

   Observations over time and possibly comparisons of performance among groups (e.g., this year's third- and fourth-year students versus the next two years').

4. What data collection measures are being used?

   The measures are achievement tests, medical record reviews, surveys.

5. What additional information do you need to perform the evaluation?
   - An explicit statement of the standards: For example, if changes are observed in quality of care, how will the adequacy of those changes be assessed?
   - An explanation and justification of the numbers and types of individuals who will participate in the evaluation: For example, how many residents and faculty will be included? Are the samples large enough to discern true differences?
   - A description of the number of observations and when they will be made
   - The data-analytic methods

CHAPTER 2

1. Evaluation questions:
    1. Have physicians learned the guidelines for transfusing red blood cells, fresh frozen plasma, platelets, and cryoprecipitated AHF?
    2. Have appropriate transfusion practices been ensured?
    3. To what extent are the guidelines associated with improved quality of care at the institution?
    4. Have all physicians benefited equally?

2. Question: Did nonphysician staff become knowledgeable about privacy issues pertaining to infectious diseases such as hepatitis and tuberculosis?

    Standards:

    - Of the staff, 80% become knowledgeable about privacy issues.
    - An improvement in knowledge is observed before and after the program (for up to 5 years) for each group of nonphysician staff.
    - A difference in knowledge is found between current and future staff in their knowledge.

    Independent variable: Staff

    Dependent variable: Knowledge

CHAPTER 3

Evaluation question 1: Has the center's quality of care improved?

Standard: The appropriateness of pain management practices improves over the 3-year program period.

Independent variables: Participation in the program

Design: An experimental evaluation with self-controls

Potential biases: During the 3-year period, a number of external events, having nothing to do with the program, may influence practice. For example, the World Health Organization or a charitable foundation might provide additional or new funds for pain management or refugees may move on or drop out of the program. A control group can guard against the influence of outside variables.

Evaluation question 2: How do patients and health care providers perceive the quality of care pertaining to the management of pain?

Standard: No judgment can be made regarding the answers to this question because it is solely for descriptive information.

Design: Survey

Potential biases: This design will provide a cross section of opinions. It cannot produce data on the extent to which the views of the responding individuals have been affected by the program or how the views compare with those held by nonparticipants.

CHAPTER 4

Answers: C, B, A.

CHAPTER 5

Answers: 1, C; 2, G; 3, A; 4, F; 5, B; 6, D; 7, E.

CHAPTER 6

1. A. The concept here is content validity because the instrument is based on a number of theoretical constructs (e.g., the Health Beliefs Model and Social Learning Theory).

   B. The concept is interrater reliability because agreement is correlated between scorers. If we also assume that each expert's ratings are true, then we have concurrent validity; k is a statistic that is used to adjust for agreements that could have arisen by chance alone.

   C. The concept is test-retest reliability because each test is scored twice.

2. See the following form:

BIRTH OUTCOME DATA FORM

Directions: This form is to be completed upon each project participant's delivery.

WHAT IS THIS MOTHER'S EVALUATION ID?	*1-4*
1. Baby's birth date:__/__/__	*5-10*
2. Birth weight: __ __ __ __ __ grams *OR* __ __ lbs __ __ ozs	*11-14*
3. Baby's sex [ ] Male [ ] Female [ ] Unknown/Could not get	*15*
4. Gestational age assessed by clinician at birth: __ weeks	*16-17*

---

5. Was drug toxicology performed at birth on the **mother** at   *18*
   delivery?

   [ ] Yes

   [ ] No

   [ ] Unknown/Not reported

5a. If **yes**, what were the results?

   [ ] Negative   *19*

   [ ] positive for alcohol   *20*

   [ ] positive for amphetamines   *21*

   [ ] positive for opiates   *22*

   [ ] positive for barbiturates   *23*

   [ ] positive for cannabinoids   *24*

   [ ] positive for cocaine or metabolites   *25*

   [ ] positive, other, specify:_____   *26*

   [ ] unknown/not reported   *27*

6. Was a drug toxicology screen performed at birth on the **baby**?   *28*

   [ ] Yes

   [ ] No

   [ ] Unknown/Not reported

   6a. If **yes**, what were the results?

   [ ] negative   *29*

   [ ] positive for alcohol   *30*

   [ ] positive for amphetamines   *31*

   [ ] positive for opiates   *32*

   [ ] positive for barbiturates   *33*

   [ ] positive for cannabinoids   *34*

   [ ] positive for cocaine or metabolites   *35*

   [ ] positive, other, specify: _____   *36*

7. What was the total number of clinical prenatal visits   *37-38*
   attended by the patient during this pregnancy?
   __ __ total prenatal care visits

8 Was the baby: [ ] stillborn   [ ] live birth   *39*

3. This information collection plan has several serious flaws. First, it only anticipates collecting data on student knowledge and skill despite the fact that the objectives also encompass attitude. Next, even if the evaluators are expert test constructors, they must pilot test and evaluate the tests to determine their reliability and validity. Finally, the evaluators do not plan to monitor the use of the educational materials. If faculty cannot or will not use them, then any results may be spurious. The 5-year plan of testing is, however, probably of sufficient duration to observe changes.

CHAPTER 7

1.

Situation	Describe independent and dependent variable.	Tell if the data are nominal, ordinal, or numerical.
Patients in the experimental and control group tell whether painkillers give complete, moderate, or very little relief.	Independent variable: group; dependent variable: pain relief	Independent variable is nominal; dependent variable is ordinal
Participants in the program are grouped according to whether they are severely, moderately, or marginally depressed and are given a survey of anxiety that is scored from 1 to 9.	Independent variable: depressed patients in the program; dependent variable: anxiety	Independent variable is ordinal; dependent variable is numerical
Children are chosen for the evaluation according to whether they have had all recommended vaccinations or not; they are followed for 5 years and their health status is monitored.	Independent variable: having or not having recommended vaccinations; dependent variable: health status	Independent variable is nominal; not enough information to tell about the dependent variable
Men and women with stage 1, 2, and 3 disease are compared in the quality of life as measured by scores ranging from 1 to 50 from standardized observations.	Independent variable: gender and stage of disease; dependent variable: quality of life	Independent variables are nominal and ordinal; dependent variable is numerical.
RNs and LVNs are surveyed, and their average proficiency scores are compared.	Independent variable: type of nurse; dependent variable: proficiency	Independent variable is nominal; dependent variable is numerical.

2. *Analysis:* A two-sample independent groups *t*-test

   Justification for the analysis: This *t*-test is appropriate when the independent variable is measured on a nominal scale and the dependent variable is measured on a numerical scale. In this case, the assumptions of a *t*-test are met. These assumptions are that each group has a sample size of at least 30, both groups' sizes are about equal, and the two groups are independent (an assumption that is met most easily with a strong evaluation design and a high-quality data collection effort).

3. If the evaluation aims to find out how younger and older persons in the experimental and control groups compare in amount of domestic violence, and presuming that the statistical assumptions are met, then an analysis of variance is an appropriate technique.

CHAPTER 8

1. Visual Aid 1 requires that the audience read too much. Also, the title of a visual should be more informative. The text suggests two visuals:

A. Stratified Random Sampling

- Population is divided into subgroups or strata.
- Random sample is selected from each stratum.

B. Stratified Random Sampling: Blueprint

Income	Age (years)			
	Under 19	20-30	31-35	Over 35
High				
Medium				
Low				

2. *Report on the table:* The table shows that, in the Opinion Leader
   Education Group (OLE), about half the women eligible for a trial of
   labor still underwent an elective cesarean section. Nevertheless, the rate
   was 21% lower than in the other groups and was significantly different
   ($P = .001$). The larger proportion of women undergoing the trial of labor
   in the OLE group did not result in significantly higher rates of
   unscheduled cesarean section ($P = .166$). This implies that physicians
   were appropriately selecting candidates for the trial of labor. Finally,
   slightly more than one half of the women eligible for a trial of labor
   were actually offered one by their physicians in the control and in the
   audit and feedback groups, whereas significantly more (74.2%) received
   the offer from physicians in OLE hospitals ($P = .002$).

Index

About the Author

ARLENE FINK (Ph.D.) is Professor of Medicine and Public Health at the University of California, Los Angeles. She is a research adviser to UCLA's Robert Wood Johnson Clinical Scholars Program, a health sciences specialist at the Veterans Administration Medical Center in Sepulveda, California, and president of Arlene Fink Associates. She has conducted evaluations throughout the United States and abroad and has trained thousands of health professionals, social scientists, and educators in program evaluation. In addition, she has published nearly 100 monographs and articles connected with evaluation methods and research. She is the coauthor of three other books in evaluation: *An Evaluation Primer, Evaluation Basics,* and *How to Conduct Surveys.*